AF530537

Trade Liberalisation and Foreign Investment in India: 1991-2001

About the book...

Prior to the launching of economic reforms in 1991, foreign trade of India suffered from strict bureaucratic controls and discretionary regulations. With a view to simplifying procedures and reducing controls, the Government made a Statement on Trade Policy in Parliament on August 13, 1991, ushering a new era in the foreign trade policy of India. Instead of controls and regulations, the focus shifted to promotion and development of foreign trade.

The present book provides a comprehensive view of the changes in India's foreign trade policy during the post-liberalisation period from 1991-2001. It also traces policy developments with regard to direct foreign investment during the reforms period. The book specifically highlights the foreign investment opportunities in promising sectors of the Indian economy.

About the author...

Vibha Mathur received her M.Phil. and Ph.D. degrees from the prestigious Department of Commerce, Delhi School of Economics, University of Delhi. She has written extensively on foreign trade and related areas. Dr. Mathur has authored two books namely, *India-European Union Trade Prospects and Impact of Euro* and *Foreign Trade of India: Policy and Developments, 1950-2000.* Her book on *Euro* has attracted considerable attention from academicians and policy makers. Dr. Mathur was a visiting fellow at the European Commission and Parliament in Brussels, Belgium in May 2001. Presently, she is a Reader in the Department of Commerce, Jesus and Mary College, University of Delhi.

Trade Liberalisation and Foreign Investment in India: 1991-2001

Vibha Mathur

NEW CENTURY PUBLICATIONS
DELHI INDIA

New Century Publications
34, Gujranwala Town, Part-2,
Delhi - 110 033 INDIA
Tel.: 7247805, 7138192
Fax: +91-11-7464774
E-mail: indiatax@del2.vsnl.net.in

Copyright © 2001 by Vibha Mathur

All rights reserved. No part of this book may be reproduced, stored in a retrieval system, or transmitted in any form or by any means, mechanical, photocopying, recording, or otherwise without the prior written permission of the publisher.

First Published 2001

ISBN: 81-7708-014-8

Published by New Century Publications and printed at Print Line, New Delhi-110 002

PRINTED IN INDIA

Preface

The year 1991 will prove to be a watershed in the economic history of modern India. It was starting this year that the Government of India introduced a series of reforms to liberalise and globalise the Indian economy. Reforms in the foreign trade sector were intended to integrate the Indian economy with the world economy.

This book traces the developments in the external sector of India, covering foreign trade and foreign direct investment, during the period 1991-2001.

Chapter 1 examines the trade policy system in India during the pre-liberalisation period. It also analyses the balance of payments crisis during the period 1950-90.

Chapter 2 is devoted to trade policy adjustments during the decade 1991-2001. Radical reforms introduced in the export-import policy of the country are also discussed.

Chapter 3 analyses trends in the commodity composition and direction of trade.

Chapter 4 reviews policy measures introduced by the Government to promote exports.

Chapter 5 describes the creation of WTO and examines its impact on the economies of developing countries, with particular emphasis on India.

Chapter 6 is devoted to policy of the Government regarding foreign direct investment.

Chapter 7 presents a sectoral analysis of foreign investment in India.

Chapter 8 highlights prospects and opportunities of foreign investment in India, with special reference to infrastructure.

I record my deep sense of gratitude to my father Dr. K.P. Mathur who has been a constant source of inspiration for me. Thanks are also due to Ms. Rekha Dayal for her encouragement and academic support while writing this book.

Lastly, I owe a special word of appreciation for my husband Dr. Alok Mathur and my children Nidhi and Vasundhara for their moral support.

Delhi
June 20, 2001

Vibha Mathur

Contents

Chapter 1

Trade Policy System in India: Pre-1991 and BOP Crisis

1.1 Introduction

International trade is an activity of strategic importance in the development process of a developing country. Foreign exchange resources provide the crucial inputs and capital goods much needed in the early stages of development. In view of the limitations in regard to the inflow of foreign aid, the twin strategies of import-substitution and export promotion assume roles of great significance in the conservation and earning of foreign exchange resources.

The strategy of import-substitution entails many questions regarding the choice of products for import-substitution, optimum degree of protection, time-phasing of the production programme etc. [1]. Similarly, strategy of expansion of export earnings also raises a number of issues such as the choice of export products, production of export goods and pricing policy.

Absence of adequate domestic resources such as capital, skilled manpower, inelasticity of demand for traditional export products, lack of mobility of factors, primitive technologies of production are some of the bottlenecks which arise in the process of rapid economic development in general. In this context, choice of suitable economic policies to harness the full development potential of the economy assumes role of strategic importance. Trade policies constitute significant part in the overall framework of economic policy and as such they deserve special attention by the policy makers.

Economic policy-making in general, is an art which requires a systematic and careful analysis of the various issues involved in it. Trade policy-making is no exception to this. Firstly, the policy-maker should lay down clearly the objectives of the policies.

Secondly, an optimum policy consistent with these objectives should be chosen. These are the ex-ante issues to be analysed before the policies are chosen. Ex-post, the policy maker should evaluate the performance of the policies in the context of the objectives for which they were chosen. This analysis should provide guidelines for future policy-making. The policy framework which has emerged from such a systematic appraisal of the past policies would be obviously a better one than that adopted without such an appraisal. A frequent review of the policies in a quantitative framework is of paramount importance.

Structure of imports and exports of a country depends among other things on the trade policies adopted by it. Trade strategy, as part of the overall plan strategy, has to be consistent with the overall objectives of the planning process. Thus in the analysis of trade structure, two related important aspects need to be analysed in a comprehensive manner. The first aspect is regarding the trade policy system in the country and the second is the relationship between the trade strategy and the plan objective.

The term trade policy refers to all the policies that have either direct or indirect bearing on the trade behaviour of a country. The details of the various policies depend upon the broad trade strategy adopted and therefore, before discussing the trade policies, the typology of the trade strategies or the trade policy systems should be identified.

1.2 Inward and Outward Orientation

It is obvious that typology of trade strategies depends upon the strategy of development adopted by the planners. For instance, if the development strategy is one of giving relatively greater emphasis on development of industry rather than that of agriculture, then the trade strategy should be suitably adopted to this development strategy. Following are the two broad strategies: 1. Inward-oriented and 2. Outward-oriented strategy.

Inward orientation is often identified with protectionism and import substitution while outward orientation with free trade and export promotion. However, in a broader framework, inward-looking and outward looking strategies my be defined to encompass wider range of activities than mere trade in goods. Inward-looking strategy may then refer to all the policies which discourage reliance on foreign resources.

Under this strategy in its extreme form, no foreign aid is permissible, no movement of factors of production to or from outside, no multi-national corporations and no freedom in international communications. Such a strategy in some form was in vogue in Russia during its Iron-Curtain Age immediately after the Second World War.

However, in the present world economy, such an extreme form of inward-orientation hardly exists in any country. The opposite of this extreme form of inward-orientation is the form of outward-orientation in which free movement of capital, labour, goods, multinational enterprises, open communications are permitted. In the present world.

economy, combinations of inward and outward orientations in different degrees are observed.

1.3 Trade Policy System in India: Pre-1991 and BOP Crisis

There have been significant reforms in the Indian economy since 1991. At least in the external sectors, these reforms have been radical enough for one to use the appellations B. R. (before reforms) and A.R. (after reforms) when referring to the Indian economy. In contrast to the external sectors, reforms in the domestic economy have been relatively tardy [2].

The period before 1991 is generally identified as an era where, barring a few exceptions, there was neglect of exports. This started in the 1950's and the early 1960s, with the Second Five Year Plan (1956-61), associated with the initiation of an inward-looking strategy of development with import substituting industrialisation as the core of the strategy. Self-reliance was adopted as a goal and trade policy often hampered exports instead of promoting them. Although export incentives were introduced prior to 1966, vigorous export promotion is identified with the period that followed the 1966 devaluation of the rupee. More specifically, the approach and policy towards exports can be divided into several distinct phases. This essentially follows the Bhagwati (1978) and Krueger (1978), Typology, which distinguishes between five phases in any process of liberalisation. In phase I, quantitative restrictions are imposed and intensified. In phase II quantitative restrictions continue, but some price measures are adopted to offset some of the undesirable effects. In phase III, attempts are made to systematise the changes of Phase II. Phase IV is associated with increased foreign exchange earnings and relaxation of quantitative restrictions, while Phase V is a regime of complete liberalisation.

Till the Second Five Year Plan, the Indian trade regime clearly belonged to Phase I. This early phase was one of extreme export pessimism, coupled with a belief in the writings of Prebisch, Singer and Nurkse. Phase II began with the Third Five Year Plan (1961-66). Although, quantitative restrictions continued, more attention was paid to exports through the setting up of export support services like export promotion councils, state trade houses and export houses and the introduction of various export subsidisation schemes. In some sense the economy moved to Phase III during 1966-68, after the 1966 devaluation. But instead of moving forward towards phase IV, the period 1968 to 1970 witnessed a movement back to phase II which lasted till at least the second half of the 1980s.

Although the 1990-91 crisis was precipitated by some short-term factors, it reflected an economic crisis that was more long-term in nature. One of the best statements of the neo-classical critique of import substitution and inward orientation is that of Little, Scitovsky and Scott (1970) and the argument readily generalises to India. In the Indian context the focus on import-substitution led to the setting up of industry at home and the industry clamoured for protection. Accordingly, industry was protected from all external competition in two ways. First, there were very high tariff rates and before the reforms started, peak tariff rates were 300 percent plus. Second, there was a complicated import-licensing regime.

Before reforms started, imports were divided into four categories - OGL (Open General Licence, which means that an import licence is not required), prohibited or banned, restricted (an import licence is required), and canalised (imports can only take place through designated state trading organisations). The import-licensing regime was so arbitrary and non-transparent that it became almost impossible to import anything, apart from distorting effective rules of protection (ERP) across sectors.

Industry was thus protected from all manner of domestic competition through an industrial licensing policy. In addition, Indian industry was protected from all manner of domestic competition through an industrial licensing policy. Thus, it faced a protected and profitable domestic market that was oligopolistic or monopolistic and had no incentive to lower costs, improve efficiency or upgrade technology.

However, this also led to a policy-induced and anti-export bias, because the world market was competitive. At the same time, one needed exports to pay for imports of raw material, capital goods, fertilisers and petroleum products. As crutches to inefficient Indian industry to go out and export, one therefore had to offer a complicated spectrum of export incentives such as the CCS (cash compensatory support) scheme and REP (replenishment licences).

Despite these export incentives, the bias in favour of producing for the domestic market was not eliminated.

1.4 Balance of Payments Crisis and Its Effects on Trade Policies

Ever since Independence in 1947, India has faced chronic deficit in its balance of payments. In other words, imports have always exceeded exports. This is not unique to India but a characteristic of most of developing and diversifying countries struggling for reconstruction and modernisation of their colonial economies.

In India, imports have galloped because of increasing requirements of capital goods, defence equipment, petroleum products, raw materials and occasionally foodgrains and edible oils. Exports have remained relatively sluggish owing to lack of exportable surplus, competition in the international market, inflation at home and increasing protectionist policies of developing countries.

1.4.1 Trends in Balance of Payments: Pre-1991

During the First Five Year Plan our balance of payments position did not indicate any sign of strain or stress with the exception of the year 1951-52, when BOP position became adverse to the extent of Rs. 162.6 crores on current account.

This favourable change at the very beginning of the plan period was due to the devaluation of the Indian rupee and also due to improvement in crop production because of climatic conditions. In the industrial sector, investment during the period was rather modest and, therefore, imports of capital goods were limited. During the Second Five Year Plan, India initiated a programme of rapid industrialisation, as a result of which imports exceeded exports and consequently an adverse balance of payments became inevitable.

Rising imports and stagnant exports led to the widening of the deficit on current account from Rs. 312.8 crores in 1956-57 to Rs. 392.4 crores in 1960-61. During the Third Five Year Plan, though a number of measures like exchange control, rigid import restrictions, maximum utilisation of foreign aid, promotion of exports and imports substitution, etc. were taken, our balance of payments situation worsened and deficit on current account jumped up from Rs. 306.4 crores in 1961-62 to Rs. 489.8 crores in 1965-66.

During three Annual Plan periods, there was a consistent and considerable trade deficit which resulted in a chronic crisis in the balance of payments. Our balance of payments showed the all-time high deficit of Rs. 812.9 crores in 1966-67, in 1968-69, the deficit was however, of Rs. 365.2 crores.

The Fourth Five Year Plan witnessed a somewhat satisfactory trend in our balance of payments position as compared to the three Annual Plans. Deficit on current account moderately increased from Rs. 445 crores in 1970-71 to Rs. 455.0 crores in 1973-74. It was in the year 1972-73 that we had an export surplus. The Fifth Five Year Plan, on the whole, showed a favourable balance of payments position. Though in 1974-75, there was a deficit of Rs. 644.4 crores, in 1975-76 there was a surplus of Rs. 294.2 crores.

Hence, from above analysis, it can be stated that the entire period (1950-51 to 1975-76) was very difficult for India's BOP, partly because of slow growth of exports in relation to import requirements and partly because of adverse external factors. This is depicted in Table 1.1.

These few years stand out as the golden years for India's BOP. India had a current account surplus (0.6 per cent of the GDP on an average) and foreign exchange reserves equivalent to about seven month's imports [3]. The satisfactory balance of payments situation in the major part of the seventies is reflected in the substantial accretion of foreign exchange reserves of the country from Rs. 438.1 crores to Rs. 5219.9 crores of rupees between 1970-71 and 1978-79, that is by almost twelve times.

During these years, export growth was good but the primary reason for the sharp improvement is net invisibles.

Table 1.1: Trends in Balance of Payments (1950-51 to 1980-81) (in Rs. crore)

	1950-51	1960-61	1970-71	1980-81
1. Imports	608	1106	1826	12544
(a) PL 480 Title 1	-	185	50	--
(b) Others	-	921	1776	12544
2. Exports (f.o.b.)	606	631	1418	6576
3. Trade balance (2-1)	-2	- 475	-408	-5967
4. Invisibles				
(a) Receipts	-	260	496	5890
(b) Payments	-	177	533	1580
(of which interest and service payments on loans and credits)		(34)	(204)	(282)
(c) Net	112.5	83	-37	4311
5. Current Account (Net)	-312*	-392	-445	-1657
6. Capital Transactions				
(a) Private				
(i) Receipts		52	80	163

Contd...

	1950-51	1960-61	1970-71	1980-81
(ii) Payments	-	35	60	66
(iii) Net	4*	17	20	97
(b) Government miscellaneous				
(i) Receipts	-	147	324	1011
(ii) Payments	-	42	353	1247
(iii) Net	-	105	-30	-236
(c) Amortisation payments (Gross)	-	-38	-232	-691
(d) Rupee Debt Service	-	-	-	-
(e) Repurchase from IMF	-6*	-11	-154	-8
(f) Banking Capital (Net)	-	10	0	13
7. Errors and Omissions	2*	-6	-67	-158
8. Total Surplus (+)/ Deficit (-) [5 to 7]	-	-316	-907	-2640
FINANCED BY :				
9. External Assistance Loans	-	257	743	1729
10. Drawls from IMF (Gross)	-	--	--	274

11. Allocation of SDRs	-	--	75	121
12. Decline(+)/Increase (-) in Reserves	-	59	89	516
TOTAL (9 TO 12)		**316**	**907**	**2640**

Source: Government of India, *Economic Survey* (Various years)

* Figures Pertain to 1956-57

Net invisibles increased from a paltry Rs. 193 crores in 1974-75 to Rs. 2486 crores in 1979-80.

The period broadly corresponds to the period of the Sixth Plan and the Seventh Plan. The external payments problem became acute in the eighties, 1980-81 through 1984-85. The trade deficit averaged Rs. 6087.2 crores of rupees per annum over this period. This was a massive increase in the trade deficit, and represented 3.4 per cent of the GDP. The current account deficit also increased sharply to an average of 2787.2 crores of rupees per annum, or 1.54 per cent of the country's GDP. However, the foreign exchange reserves increased steadily in 1984-85.

The deficit on external trade and payments suddenly jumped from the first year of the Seventh Plan and was particularly acute during the last two years of the plan (1980-90). The BOP crisis can be traced to the cumulative effect of a number of factors, among which the more important factors are (i) widening trade deficits, (ii) gradual decline in net receipts from invisibles and (iii) reduction inflows of concessional assistance to India.

Table 1.2 presents a summary view of the BOP for the years 1990-91 to 2000-2001. The developments in India's trade and payments over these years mark a noticeable structural change towards a more stable and sustainable balance of payments. During the post-liberalisation period, there had been a sharp improvement in the coverage of import payments through export earnings. The coverage ratio had averaged around 88 per cent since 1992-93, compared with only 52.4 per cent at the beginning of the 1980's and about 70 per cent at the end of the 1980's. There had also been a marked improvement in the flow of invisible receipts. Together these changes brought about a sharp

Table 1.2: Trends in Balance of Payments (1990-91 to 2000-2001)

(in Rs. crores)

	1990-91	1994-95	1995-96	1996-97	1997-98	1998-99	1999-2000	2000-2001*
1. Imports (c.i.f.)	50086	112748	146542	173756	190266	204439	240112	280600
2. Exports (f.o.b)	33152	84328	108481	121193	129515	147481	165993	203780
3. Trade Balance (2-1)	-16933	-28420	-38061	-52559	-60750	-56958	-74119	-76820
4. Invisibles								
(a) Receipts	13393	48838	59481	76533	85517	108460	131498	NA
(b) Payments	13828	31001	41027	39813	49321	69769	75378	NA
(of which: Interest and service payments on loans & credits	(4958)	(8446)	(7734)	(7813)	(10416)	(12851)	(13811)	NA
(c) Net	-434	17837	18416	36279	36922	38691	56120	50600
5. Current account (net)	-17369	-10583	-19645	-16281	-20883	-16787	-17999	-26220
6. Capital Account								
i) Foreign Investment	183	15087	15623	20720	18432	9737	22184	NA

a) Inflow	201	18085	19041	27342	33045	24825	53125	NA
b) Outflow	18	2998	3418	6621	14612	15088	30941	NA
c) Net	183	15087	15623	20720	18432	9737	22184	NA
ii) Loans	9927	9542	7974	16981	17457	18863	6951	NA
- External Assistance								
a) Inflow	6094	10029	10101	10892	10827	11508	13342	NA
b) Outflow	2140	5256	6799	6923	7441	8107	9471	NA
c) Net	3954	4773	3302	3969	3386	3401	3871	3680
- Commercial Borrowings								
a) Inflow	10827	24299	28294	52097	53315	50363	43304	NA
b) Outflow	4854	19530	23622	39084	39246	34901	40224	NA
c) Net	5973	4769	4671	13012	14069	15462	3080	NA
iii) Banking								
a) Receipts	18133	22033	21691	28394	33056	34547	48774	NA
b) Payments	16908	23091	19246	20504	36243	28169	36995	NA
c) Net	1224	-1058	2445	7890	-3187	6379	11779	NA
iv) Rupee Debt Service	-2139	-3089	-3105	-2542	-2783	-3308	-3059	-3220

v) Other Capital								
a) Receipts	5593	6911	2474	9390	14458	16563	17416	NA
b) Payments	2128	700	11140	10267	9171	11879	10881	NA
c) Net	3464	6211	-8666	-876	5287	4684	6535	NA
vi) Errors and Omissions	236	2049	1286	-2114	931	-1323	1379	NA
7.. Total Capital (i to vi)	12897	28742	15558	40501	37536	35032	45769	NA
8. Overall Balance(5+7)	-4470	18159	-4048	24220	16653	18245	27770	NA
9. Monetary Movement								
a) IMF Transactions								
- Purchases	333	-	-	-	-	NA	NA	NA
- Repurchases	1155	3585	5749	3461	2286	1652	1122	NA
- Net	2177	-3585	-5749	-3461	-2286	-1652	-1122	NA
b) Increase (-)/ decrease (+) in Reserves	2293	-14574	9797	-20758	-14367	-16593	-26648	NA
10. Total (a+b)	4470	-18159	4048	-24220	-16653	-18245	-27770	NA

* Provisional ; Note: Data from 1990-91 onwards are based on revised format as adopted by the RBI.

Sources: 1. RBI, *Report on Currency and Finance, 1999-2000;* 2. *Economic Survey, 2000-2001*, Ministry of Finance, Government of India; 3. CMIE, *Monthly Review of the Indian conomy*, May 2001.

reduction in the ratio of the current account deficit to GDP, from an unsustainable level of 3.2 per cent in 1990-91 to 0.8 per cent in 1994-95.

There had also been a structural change in the current account in terms of a sharp reduction in debt creating flows and an increased recourse to non-debt creating foreign investment flows. This declining trend was shared by all the major components of debt flows, namely, external assistance, commercial borrowing and non-resident deposits. This favourable shift, away from recourse to debt creating flows for financing the current account deficit, had obvious implications for moderating and reducing future debt service liability.

The BOP situation in 1996-97 and in 1997-98 remained manageable, despite some concerns on the export front. Export growth slowed down significantly because of international and domestic factors. Import growth also decelerated on account of continued industrial slackness. Net inflow on the invisibles account surged and reached a new peak in 1996-97.

The deficit on the current account of balance of payments declined to 1.0 per cent of GDP in 1996-97 from 1.8 per cent of GDP in 1995-96. The capital account of balance of payments exhibited a handsome surplus in 1996-97, following sustained buoyancy in foreign investment flows and a surge in net inflow of non-resident deposits.

The rupee was fairly stable during 1996-97 vis-à-vis the US dollar, it moved in a narrow range of Rs. 34.24 (April 1996) and Rs. 35.87 (March 1997). The stability in the exchange rate of the rupee was disturbed in the last week of August 1997, when the currency experienced a mild contagion effect of currency turmoil in Southeast Asia.

India's balance of payments withstood fairly well the turbulence in the international economic and financial markets. In fact, the balance of payments in 1997-98 remained comfortable with substantial reserve accumulation for the second year in succession, supported by strong private capital flows. Export growth has slowed down sharply over the last three years because of both international and domestic factors. Total import growth also decelerated. Net inflows on the invisibles account was buoyant in 1997-98, benefiting from sustained growth in software exports.

The deficit on the current account of the balance of payments widened to US $ 6.5 billion or 1.6 per cent of GDP in 1997-98 from 1.1 per cent of GDP in 1996-97. The BOP situation had been manageable in 1998-99, despite the continuing slowdown of exports and a marked deceleration in capital flows. Table 1.2 gives some projections for the year 2000-2001.

1.4.2 Exports Surge During 2000-2001

The provisional data available shows that exports reached at $ 44.2 billion during 2000-2001. This reflects a robust growth of 17.6 per cent over the provisional exports of $ 37.6 billion in 1999-2000.

The growth during 2000-2001 is comparable for the period 1993-94 to 1995-96 when exports witnessed fantastic growth in the range of 19 to 21 per cent.

1.5 Conclusions

The problem of deficits in BOP has come to stay with us for long now. All through the nearly five decades of planning, India has been running a deficit on the balance of payments. Initially, the extent and nature of these deficits was not very unfavourable as (i) the size of the deficits was not alarming and (ii) a large part of the deficit on current account was caused by a deficit on balance of trade and was financed by external assistance.

It was expected that the deficits on the BOP would be totally wiped out or considerably toned down as the economy progressed. But our hopes have been belied and the BOP crisis has continued during the last five decades. Many factors have been responsible for this situation. Among which are a frequent hike in the prices of crude oil and inflationary rise in prices of other import commodities.

The Government has taken several important steps to reduce the BOP crisis by enhancing exports and introducing a new import-export tariff policy in 1991. Strategies to promote exports included Full Convertibility of the rupee, various liberalisation measures undertaken with regard to industrial and trade practices and greater emphasis was laid on high value items like ready-made garments, leather goods and finished steel, etc.

Another important step taken by the Government in this direction was the introduction of Foreign Trade (Development and Regulation) Act in 1992 which replaced the Import and Export (Control) Act, 1947. This Act of 1992 empowered the Central Government to formulate and announce from time to time the Export and Import policy and to amend it in like manner.

The encouraging factor is that during the period 2000-2001 a healthy export growth was witnessed. The growth remained in the range of 15-30 per cent during each month, only exception being November 2000 when exports had increased by relatively lower rate of 6.3 per cent. However, with visible deceleration in US economy and expected unfavourable conditions in many countries, which are India's major export markets, the Indian exporters would be facing a majoı challenge to maintain the high growth recorded during 2000-2001 in the year 2001-2002.

Notes

1. Panchmukhi, V.R.: *Trade Policies of India - A Quantitative Analysis*: Concept Publishing House, 1978.

2. Debroy, Bibek: *'50 years of Independence: 1947-97, Status, Growth and Development'*; B.R. Publishing Corporation, 1998.

3. Da Costa, G.C.; *India's Balance of Payments in the Seventies and the Eighties* (Himalaya Publishing House, 1990).

Chapter 2

Trade Policy System : 1991-2001

2.1 Trade Policy Adjustments in India: Post-1991

Trade policy in India has been subject to significant changes since the beginning of the last decade. The Alexander Committee on trade policy appointed by the Ministry of Commerce (MOC) had suggested in 1978 an overhauling of India's import and export control policies, especially through delicensing of imports. An official committee on trade policy headed by P. Tandon came up in 1982 with recommendations for a package of export promotional measures which included subsidies and fiscal concessions to exporters [1].

Supplementary measures were recommended by the Abid Hussain Committee of 1984 on import and export policies which reiterated the need for trade policy reforms, for achieving both improved trade balance and efficiency in resource use. Stress was laid on export promotion, import liberalisation and especially on a greater access to free flow of technology from abroad, presumably by means of an earlier access to foreign equity participation in India. It was claimed that a freer flow of foreign direct investment (FDI) would contribute to higher exports, possibly by ushering in technological innovations in the export sector.

Recommendations offered by the three official Committee reports were sought to be implemented in the annual and the long-term import and export (LTMX) policy announcements of the MOC during the ensuing years. The first two long-term policy statements covered the financial years 1985-86 to 1987-88 and 1988-89 to 1990-91. Changes in the political regime at the Centre prompted the interruption of the on-going policy by a new LTMX policy in March 1990 covering 1990-91 to 1992-93.

In quick succession a set of supplementation, short-term trade measures were also announced especially after July 1991, when a package of economic reforms was launched by the newly elected government. A fresh LTMX policy was announced in April 1992, covering 1992-93 to 1996-97. Emphasis placed in the earlier policy announcements on import liberalisation and export promotions continued, along with a simplification of the prevailing licensing devices.

Looking back at the trade policy reforms initiated over the last few years, recommendations offered by the three trade policy committees seem to have influenced the broad goals of the successive LTMX policies, announced respectively in March 1985 to March 1988, March 1990 and April, 1992. A general move towards liberalisation of imports, especially of capital goods and raw materials, and an emphasis on export incentives (provided through preferential import licenses) seem to have dominated the major trade policy reforms.

Implementation of trade policy in India, however, has been subject to frequent short-run adjustments, especially since March 1990. These short-run measures were in the nature of deviations from LTMX goals, and designed to combat the critical external payments situation faced by the nation during these years. As could be expected, the short-run or medium-term difficulties on the balance of payments front initiated these temporary deviations from the long-run path of liberalisation and delicensing of imports.

Several of these were announced in quick succession after March 1990 when India faced a critical external payments situation. While the LTMX announcements spelt out the broad parameters in India's trade policy, the ad-hoc short-term changes were geared to the immediate problem of financing imports. The broad policies of the LTMX policies, enunciated at the beginning of this section, provided the general guidelines of the different trade policy announcements of the Ministry of Commerce, which also aimed to tackle the short-term exigencies. Such efforts clearly generated sources of deviations from the long-term directions in India's trade policy.

During the first eight months of the fiscal year 1990-91, two tendencies in the different measures adopted, were noticed. First, a general move towards delicensing of imports and reductions in customs tariffs, the former entailing successive expansions in the OGL list (Open General Licensing). Second, an attempt to link up export promotional efforts to import liberalisation, by issuing import licenses and concessions which are exclusively granted to exporters.

In October, 1992, special import licenses were issued to exporters which enabled them to import items on the restricted list and also 18 consumer items from the negative list. Transferability of these licenses, issued on an actual user basis, provided additional incentives to the exporters, especially as long as they fetched high premiums on the market. This was in contrast to the practice in the non-traded manufacturing sector which received only non-transferable supplementary licenses.

A steady pace of delicensing of imports and reduction of average customs tariffs since 1990 reduced the special privileges enjoyed by the export sector through REP [Restrictive Export-Import] (later EXIM), and other export-linked import licenses. Special efforts, however, were made to retain the incentives for exports by means of the Export Promotion Capital Goods (EPCG) scheme and other devices in the LTMX announcement of April 1992.

Long-run tendencies towards liberalisation were also evident in March 1990 LTMX package. With 182 new items added to the existing OGL list and increased value limits for supplementary licenses, the target of linking import licenses to export earning could only be designed with a set of export-oriented licensing measures. An abiding interest in protecting domestic manufacturing however, seems to have influenced the decision to shift 153 capital goods items from the OGL to the restricted list in April 1991 on grounds of domestic availability and essentiality. Similarly, in December 1991, 34 items were shifted from the OGL to the limited permissible list. Short-run deviations such as these from the long-run goals surfaced in trade policy during 1990-91 and 1991-92.

Often the changes were of short duration, reflecting the contingent and ad hoc pattern of these arrangements. The fact remains that these measures were devised to combat the short-run exigencies, especially relating to foreign exchange availability. The decline in the stock of India's official reserves reached alarming proportions by the third quarter of 1990.

Different moves were launched during the second half of 1990 and the calendar year 1991 to restrain the flow of import payments which would otherwise have assumed much higher proportions because of the on-going process of import liberalisation. Steps to reduce imports included the 15 percent cut, in July, 1990 in the value of the free foreign exchange component of supplementary licenses issued, on an 18-month basis. These industries evidently made use of the REP route to import, which was permissible to them. In November 1990, they were also allowed the OGL (actual user) route, a step which sought to correct the earlier square of 1990 on supplementary licences, especially since the OGL as previously denied to those who enjoyed supplementary licences.

The waves in the direction of liberalisation seem to have been temporarily arrested as grants of fresh licences were virtually stopped in November 1990, and import licences were subject to fresh screening. Imports of capital goods, however, were exempt from these stipulations, probably with an anticipated lag of at least six months before licences were actually utilised. Fresh circulars were issued in December 1990 which virtually stopped all foreign exchange out-go including that on imports of capital goods. In an important announcement in November 1990, the RBI directed the commercial banks to charge higher cash margins and higher interest rates for financing imports of capital goods. Cash margin requirements were tightened further during March-May 1991. Imports of capital goods, POL, and other essential consumer items including imports by public sector undertakings were excluded from the cash margin requirements.

Successive increases in cash margin requirements announced in quick succession provided a clear signal to importers that henceforth it would be advisable not to place an order for imports unless they were in a position to look in the cash stipulated for an average period of at least three months. Direct imports of capital goods, however, were permissible, irrespective of their values, provided credit lines with financial institutions (like ICICI) could be opened.

The REP licences which alone could be used to obtain importables under the limited permissible list continued to expand as items were subsequently transferred to OGL from the restricted list. The replacement in July 1991 of the differentiated REP structure (which ranged between 5 and 20 percent of the f.o.b. value of exports) by EXIM (which were pitched at a uniform 30 percent f.o.b. value of exports) was recognised as a major step in the direction of export-oriented import liberalisation. Prior to 1991, tariff rates in India were very high and the tariff system was also quite complicated. In mid-1991 when the new Government assumed office at the Centre, it began the process of reducing import duties.

Radical reforms were introduced in the Indian customs tariff between 1991 and 1997. These reforms were necessary because the customs tariff had become, over the years, very complicated in terms of multiple rates, innumerable exemptions, excessive controls, and elaborate procedures. These infirmities of the customs tariff often led to delays, harassment, corruption and litigation. Moreover, rationalisation and simplification of the customs duties was needed to move towards a market economy, freedom of trade and opening up the Indian economy to the outside world. The major changes included the following: (i) the peak rate of import duty was reduced from 200 per cent to 40 per cent, (ii) average rate of import duty was scaled down from 50 per cent to 25 per cent, (iii) import duty on capital goods was brought down from 85 per cent to 25 per cent. The country has moved towards moderate rates of taxation with a view to improve compliance and reduce litigation.

2.1.1 Move Towards Liberalised EXIM Policies

India's foreign trade is regulated by the Foreign Trade (Development and Regulation) Act, 1992 which replaced the Import and Export (Control) Act, 1947. The Act of 1992 empowers the Central Government to formulate and announce from time to time the export and import policy and to amend it in like manner.

Prior to mid-1991, foreign trade of India suffered from strict bureaucratic and discretionary controls. However, the new Government which took over at the centre in June, 1991 soon realised that India's foreign trade policy must respond to the changes (liberalisation and openness) sweeping across the world. To reduce controls, simplify procedures and to create a congenial environment for trade, the Government made a statement on Trade Policy in Parliament on August 13, 1991, ushering a new era in the foreign trade policy of India. Instead of controls and regulations, the focus shifted to promotion and development of foreign trade.

Before 1985-86, the annual export import policy was announced at the beginning of the financial year. In 1985-86, a three year export-import policy was announced for the period April 1985 through March 1988, providing a reasonable degree of stability to the policy framework. On its expiry, the new policy for three years 1988-91 was announced in March 1988 which laid even greater emphasis on promotion of exports.

On 1st April, 1992, a comprehensive export promotion scheme was launched under the Export Promotion Capital Goods Scheme (EPCG) along with value added advance licences which provided the exporters concessional and duty-free access to the respective imports of capital goods, raw materials and components. Similarly, the EPZ/EOU schemes were extended to cover agricultural operations, with facilities for duty-free imports of all inputs.

In a significant move the LTMX of April 1992 also changed the basis of concessionary import facilities granted to the EOU/EPZs from NFEE (Net Foreign Exchange Earnings) to f.o.b. value of physical exports. Facilities for concessional imports were also extended to the services sector as professionals offering services to foreign tourists in India received benefits under the EPCG scheme against earnings in foreign currency. All these measures clearly sought to forge and fortify the links between imports and exports.

Moves to strengthen liberalisation measures in the economy were marked in the budget of 1992-93 which introduced a simplification of import licensing procedures by scrapping the multiple lists of imports. Customs duties on imports of a large variety of items were slashed in the budget of 1993-94 which reduced the peak average duty from 110 percent to 85 percent. Selective measures to delicense imports included the May 1993 measures to dispense with the negative list for imports of finished drugs. Pressures, both domestic and external, seem to have initiated, once again, the short-run deviations even in the new LTMX policy of 1992-97. Thus, indigenous inputs were excluded from the computation of value addition for export obligations of the EOU/EPZ units, a step devised to encourage the use of indigenous inputs by the latter. Later in June 1993, counter-veiling duties were imposed on a range of products, on the grounds that it would create a level playing field for both the importer and the domestic manufacturer of such goods.

2.1.2 Export-Import Policy, 1992-97: An Evaluation

On March 31, 1992, the Government announced the Export and Import Policy for a period of five years (April 1, 1992 to March 31, 1997), coinciding with the period of Eighth Five Year Plan. The Chief Controller of Imports and Exports was redesignated as Directorate General of Foreign trade. Export and Import Policy, 1992-97 made a conscious effort to dismantle various protectionist and regulatory policies and accelerate India's transition towards a globally oriented economy. The EXIM policy was further liberalised by the Government on March 31, 1993. Substantial concessions had been announced to boost agricultural exports. The Government had also announced a centrally sponsored scheme to set up industrial parks in different states.

Major reforms in trade policy and procedures since the announcement in March 1992 of the EXIM Policy for 1992-97, had accelerated India's transition towards a globally oriented economy by stimulating exports and facilitating imports of essential inputs as well as capital goods.

One of the main objectives of the EXIM Policy-1992-97 and changes therein during the last four years was to phase out quantitative restrictions in the form of licensing and other discretionary controls [2].

Thus, in 1991 imports were regulated by means of a positive list of freely importable items. Since 1992 imports are regulated through a limited negative list.

- Quantitative restrictions on imports of most intermediate inputs and capital goods had been eliminated.

- In July 1991 out of 5021 harmonised system (H.S.) tariff lines (6 digits), 80 per cent i.e. 4000 lines were subject to import licensing restrictions. As of December 1995, more than 3000 tariff lines covering raw materials, intermediate and .capital goods were free of import licensing requirements.

- A large number of items covering 1,487 tariff lines whose import was otherwise restricted, were allowed to be imported under freely tradable Special Import Licences.

- Through continuous review and revisions during the last four years, control on exports were liberalised to the extent that almost all goods were exported without any restriction except the few items mentioned in the negative list of exports. The items in the negative list are regulated because of strategic considerations, environmental and ecological grounds, essential domestic requirement employment generation and on grounds of socio-cultural heritage.

It will be fallacious to read the exim policy as an independent document and arrive at interpretations based on this. It has to be interpreted along with changes in the policies vis-à-vis foreign exchange, taxation and the other trade reforms that had taken place prior to the release of the new EXIM policy document - the scrapping of export subsidies, allowing exporters to retain a part of their foreign exchange earnings, the devaluation of the rupee, partial convertibility of the rupee and the creation of an official open market for foreign exchange.. These policy changes implied that from an active interventionist policy in the foreign trade regime, the government set up the broader macro-economic parameters and let the market decide the exact volume and value of foreign trade.

On the positive side, the new export-import policy had been declared as bold, innovative and balanced.

1. The policy made both imports and exports free, subject to negative lists and filled in with the market driven

system expected to globalise the economy.

2. The decision to give special import licences to export houses, trading houses and star trading houses has resulted in boosting exports.

3. The decision to permit EOUs and EPZs to exports through these houses strengthened the operations of these professional exporting firms as well as EOUs and EPZs.

4. The decision to take corrective measures to encourage deemed exports have helped in conserving foreign exchange.

5. The introduction of two tier system of concessional customs duty of 25 per cent and 15 per cent also provided a good stimulus to exports through technological renovation.

2.1.3 Export-Import Policy, 1997-2002: A Critical Review

The Export and Import Policy, 1997-2002 (coinciding with the period of Ninth Five Year Plan) seeks to consolidate the gains of the previous policy and further carry forward the process of liberalisation by deregulating and simplifying procedures and removing quantitative restrictions in a phased manner. It has set an ambitious target of attaining an export level of US $ 90-100 billion by the year 2002 and achieving 1 per cent share in world trade.

Objectives and Salient Features

The principal objectives of the policy are the following:

1. To accelerate the country's transition to a globally oriented vibrant economy with a view to derive maximum benefits from expanding global market opportunities.

2. To stimulate sustained economic growth by providing access to essential raw materials, intermediates, components, consumables and capital goods required for augmenting

production.

3. To enhance the technological strength and efficiency of Indian agriculture, industry and services, thereby improving their competitive strength while generating new employment opportunities, and encourage the attainment of internationally accepted standard of quality.

4. To provide consumers with good quality products at reasonable prices.

Following are the salient features of the policy:

(a) Exports and imports shall be free, except to the extent they are regulated by the provisions of this policy.

(b) The Central Government may, in public interest, regulate the import or export of goods by means of a negative list of imports or a negative list of exports, as the case may be.

(c) The Negative Lists may consist of goods, the import or export of which is prohibited, restricted through licensing, or canalised. The Negative List of Imports and the Negative List of Exports are contained in the policy.

(d) Prohibited items in the Negative List of Imports shall not be imported and prohibited items in the Negative List of Exports shall not be exported.

(e) Any goods, the export or import of which is restricted through licensing, may be exported or imported only in accordance with a licence issued in this behalf.

(f) Any goods, the import or export of which is canalised, may be imported or exported by the canalising agency specified in the Negative List.

(g) No export or import shall be made by any person without an Importer-Exporter Code (IEC) number unless specifically exempted.

2.1.4 Export-Import Policy 1999-2000: The Millennium Agenda

In its effort to further dismantle the import control regime and hasten the integration of the Indian economy with the world economy, the Government announced a revised export-import policy on March 31 1999 which came into force on April 1, 1999.

The new export-import policy freed import of 894 items of consumer goods, agricultural products and textiles from licensing requirements. In other words, a number of consumer items could now be imported license-free subject only to the payment of import duty. Physical controls on imports were removed and the only control over imports was fiscal in nature, i.e. adjusting import duty to regulate imports. These adjustments were to be made within the upper limits prescribed by WTO.

Moreover, another 414 items were removed from the *restricted list*, allowing these to be imported against special import licenses. India's international commitments require it to remove licensing curbs on imports by the year 2003.

2.1.5 Export-Import Policy, 2000-2001: Radical Reforms

The Union Commerce and Industry Minister announced on March 31, 2000 the new Export-Import Policy of the Government of India for the year 2000-2001. The export-import policy, envisaging a 20 per cent export growth in dollar terms in 2000-2001, brought about a major rationalisation in export promotion schemes and launched a series of sector-specific initiatives.

A. Export Promotion: In a major initiative to boost exports, the Government announced the following measures:

Special Economic Zones (SEZs): On the pattern of the

Chinese model, the Government announced the setting up of two SEZs, at Positra in Gujarat and Nangunery in Tamil Nadu. Industrial units located in SEZs will be exempted from a plethora of rules and regulations governing exports and imports. The entire production will have to be exported from these zones. Sales from Domestic Tariff Area (DTA) can be done only on full payment of customs duty. Several Export Processing Zones (EPZs) will shortly be converted into SEZs. The EPZs located in Kandla, Vizag and Kochi will be converted into SEZs immediately. It was further announced that 100 per cent foreign direct investment (FDI) would be allowed in all products in SEZs.

SEZs would be treated as if they are outside the customs territory of the country. The units would be able to import capital goods and raw materials duty free. The movement of goods to and from SEZs would be unrestricted. A fiscal incentive package (including tax holiday) for export units to be located in SEZs would be announced by the Government in due course.

It is noteworthy that SEZs have played a crucial role in boosting China's exports and presently the country derives 40 per cent of its exports from such zones. However, Chinese SEZs are based on contract labour system (hire and fire policy). The Commerce Minister while announcing the EXIM Policy categorically rules out any changes in labour laws. Moreover, there is no system of reservation of items for small-scale industries in China. It is unclear if the Government of India would allow the production of reserved items for small industries in the SEZs.. Still further, there are various infrastructural bottlenecks like power shortage, lack of transport facilities and of course procedural delays. Hence, the success of SEZs in India is a moot question.

Sector-specific Packages: The Export-Import Policy 2000-2001 announced sector-specific packages for seven core areas to boost exports, viz. gems and jewellery, pharmaceuticals, agro-chemicals, biotechnology, silk, leather and garments.

For the gems and jewellery exporters, the Government announced a diamond-dollar account (DDA) scheme. Under the scheme, export proceeds can be retained in a dollar account and the exporters can use funds in this account for import of rough diamonds.

For agro-chemicals, biotechnology and pharma units (considered as knowledge-intensive), the Government has allowed duty-free import of laboratory equipment, chemicals and reagents up to 1 per cent of the FOB value of exports. Similarly, the Government increased duty-free import of trimmings, embellishments and other items from 2 to 3 per cent of total export values.

Involvement of State Governments in Export Promotion: Since the States forgo taxes (mainly sales tax) on exports, they have little incentive to promote exports. The 2000-2001 Export-Import Policy announced financial incentives to States based on their export performance. An incentive scheme with an initial outlay of Rs. 250 crore to secure States' involvement in the national export drive was unveiled. The States can use the funds for export promotion activities such as infrastructure development. The Commerce and Industry Minister said that he would request the States to treat all units exporting more than 50 per cent of their turnover as public utility services. This would enable them to keep their international commitment on delivery schedules.

Furthermore, the Minister observed that the recent

spectacular growth of software exports was, apart from India's knowledge in high-tech, due to hands off policy of the Government towards this sector. A similar approach to hardware electronics is called for.

B. Import Liberalisation: The Export-Import Policy 2000-2001 lifted quantitative restrictions on 714 commonly used items (agricultural products and consumer durables) which can now be freely imported. Thus, commodities like meat, milk powder, coffee, tea, fish, pickles, cigars and cigarettes, televisions, radios, tape recorders, footwear and umbrellas can be imported freely from April 1, 2000. However, most of these items will attract peak rate of basic import duty of 35 per cent which when increased with surcharge and special customs duty will add up to a total of 44 per cent in import duties. Furthermore, the 44 per cent will be enhanced by countervailing duty equivalent to domestic excise duty on the product being imported.

The lifting of licensing and quota restrictions on 714 import items was in line with India's WTO obligations. The Government promised to abolish licensing and quota curbs on the remaining 715 items (such as liquor, cars etc.) in April 2001.

Many critics of the new policy fear that removal of licensing and quota restrictions would lead to surge in imports of these items, hurting the domestic industry. However, it is noteworthy that import restrictions are being phased out since 1996 but no extraordinary growth has occurred in the import of freed items. The Commerce Minister maintained that anti-dumping and anti-subsidy tariffs and other safeguards would be used if there is a sudden surge in imports, causing serious injury to the domestic industry.

2.2 Export-Import Policy, 2001-2002: Outlook for the 21st Century

The Union Commerce and Industry Minister unveiled on March 31, 2001, the Export-Import Policy for the year 2001-2002.

A. Removal of Quantitative Restrictions: The process of removal of import restrictions, which began in 1991, was completed in a phased manner by the Export-Import Policy 2001-2002 with the removal of restrictions on the remaining 715 items. This was in tune with the commitments made to the WTO. Out of these 715 items, 342 were textile products, 147 were agricultural products and 226 were other manufactured products.

However, import of agricultural products like wheat, rice, maize, copra and coconut oil was placed in the category of State Trading. The nominated State Trading Enterprise will conduct the import of these commodities solely as per commercial considerations. Similarly, import of petroleum products including petrol, diesel and ATF was placed in the category of State Trading. In all 27 out of 715 items taken off the quantitative restrictions list were put under the State Trading category.

The Minister was confident that the Indian market will not be swamped by imported brands of commonly used articles. To prevent dumping, Government will take recourse to anti-dumping duties and other non-tariff barriers. arrangements have been made to track, collate and analyse data on 300 sensitive items which mainly comprise farm goods and items produced by small scale sector.

B. Agricultural Export Zones: With a view to boost agricultural exports and provide remunerative returns to the farming community, the Export-Import Policy proposed the setting up of agricultural export zones. Three such zones are proposed to be set up in Himachal Pradesh, Jammu and Kashmir (to promote export of apples) and Maharashtra. Government will make efforts to provide improved access to the produce/products of the agriculture and allied sectors in the international market. State Governments have been asked to identify product specific agricultural export zones for development for export of specific products from a geographically contiguous area.

2.3 Tariff Policy, 1991-2001: A Review

In India, about 99 per cent of customs revenue is derived from import duties which are levied on a wide range of commodities. In the 2000-2001 budget, the share of customs revenue in Centre's total tax collections was estimated at 24.2 per cent. Apart from revenue function, import duties act as policy instrument to provide protection to domestic industry, conserve and ration scarce foreign exchange, and frame external trade policy of the Government. Export duties, accounting for the rest of 1 per cent revenue, are imposed on a few commodities, namely coffee, mica, black pepper, hides and skins, and leather. Government has generally refrained from levying export duties in order to ensure competitiveness of India's exports in the world market.

2.3.1 Lowering of Import Tariff

The need for import tariff rationalisation was underlined in the Long Term Fiscal Policy (LTFP) Statement of the Government, 1985. The official document noted that the prevailing tariff rates were high and the tariff system was very complicated. Therefore, it stressed the need to reduce the rates and simplify the system. For carrying out these reforms, the LTFP distinguished between the following broad categories of imports: (i) capital goods, (ii) raw materials, (iii) other intermediate goods including components, (iv) essential consumer goods like foodgrains, edible oils, and life saving drugs and (v) non-essential consumer goods. Understandably, essential goods were preferred to either remain exempt or bear low rates of import duties while non-essential items were singled out to either remain banned or subjected to high import tariff.

First, the substitution of the present multiplicity of nominal tariff rates by a single rate would constitute an enormous simplification for both trade and industry as well as for the customs administration. Second, this would vastly reduce incentives for misclassification of imports to evade taxes. Third, a single nominal rate of import duty would assure a uniform rate of effective protection (that is, protection of value added) at different stages of production of intermediate and capital goods. This would encourage the economy to specialise in those activities in which it has competitive strength." [3].

However, the LTFP cautioned that a major deviation from the then existing pattern of import tariff was not immediately feasible. Domestic industries had grown under different levels of protection and were in different stages of maturity. The rationalisation of import tariff had to be phased over a long period providing some differentials in import tariff short of a uniform system of duties.

Consequent upon the rationalisation of import tariff on capital goods by the Finance Act, 1987, the rate of import duty on general machinery was reduced to 85 per cent *ad valorem*. Import duty on components for machinery was fixed at 15 per cent below the applicable rate on complete machines. This differential was intended to encourage the domestic production of capital machines instead of their total imports. Imports of capital goods for certain preferred sectors were allowed at relatively low rates of duty. For example, duty on equipment for fertiliser plants was 15 per cent *ad valorem* and on machines, equipment, and tools for gem and jewellery 25 per cent *ad valorem*. Electronics industry emerged as a preferred sector for fiscal incentives.

The Finance Act, 1988, fixed a uniform concessional import duty of 60 per cent *ad valorem* in respect of 280 items of machinery for the electronics sector. By the same Act, the duty on moulds, tools, and dies required by the electronics industry was reduced from 60 per cent to 30 per cent *ad valorem* with the underlying purpose of indigenisation and development of electronics and computers.

In short, reforms in import tariff structure were never implemented comprehensively and only in case of some industries rationalisation of rates were effected like components of capital goods, drug intermediates, and electronic goods.

In mid-1991 when the new Government assumed office at the Centre, it began the process of reducing import duties. The Finance Act (No. 2), 1991, reduced the *ad valorem* rate of basic plus auxiliary duties of customs to a maximum of 150 per cent where it was more than that. Thus, tariff peaks above 150 per cent were eliminated with the exceptions of duty on imported alcoholic beverages and passenger baggage. The then prevailing rates of import duty on capital goods for general projects and machinery were reduced from 85 per cent to 80 per cent. The rate of duty on their components was also reduced by 5 percentage points from the existing level of 65 per cent.

2.3.2 Tax Reforms Committee, 1991

Reform of the customs tariff was high on the agenda of the Tax Reforms Committee (TRC), 1991. Its terms of reference enjoined it to examine and make recommendations, *inter alia*, on "simplification and rationalisation of customs tariffs with a view to reducing the multiplicity and dispersion of rates and to eliminate exemptions which have become unnecessary; (and) reducing the level of tariff rates, keeping in view the need for mobilising resources to facilitate fiscal adjustment and the objective of promoting international competitiveness." [4].

In its Interim Report submitted to the Government in December 1991, the Committee suggested the following as elements of the programme of import tariff reform, "(a) reduction of the general level of tariff, (b) reduction of the spread or dispersion of tariff rates, (c) simplification of the tariff system, (d) rationalisation of tariff rates, along with the abolition of numerous exemptions and concessions and (e) abolition of the practice of making changes in effective rates through notifications.". Stressing the need for time-bound action, the Committee observed, "By 1995-96, the average tariff rate should be brought down to about 50 per cent and the peak rate to about 80 per cent. In the years 1996-97 to 1998-99, tariff rates should be reduced further to bring down the average rate to around 25 per cent and the maximum rate to 50 per cent by 1998-99."

Following the recommendations of the TRC, the Finance Act, 1992, lowered the peak level of import duties to 110 per cent with the exception of passenger baggage and alcoholic beverages. With a view to reduce the cost of new investment, the duty on project imports was lowered from 80 per cent to 55 per cent and in the case of electronic industry to 50 per cent. A deeper reduction to 30 per cent was granted for capital goods for projects of coal mining and crude petroleum refining. For power projects, a uniform duty of 30 per cent was fixed.

The underlying philosophy of reduction in tariffs was to promote competitiveness in the Indian industry. There was a feeling in Government circles that high tariff rates had the effect of creating a high cost industrial structure.

The Finance Act, 1993, made a significant simplification in the import tariff by merging auxiliary duty with basic duty, and also by reducing the maximum rate of import duty from 110 per cent to 85 per cent. The peak rate of import duty was further reduced from 85 per cent to 65 per cent by the Finance Act, 1994.

Continuing the process of reducing the high level of protection to domestic industry to foster competition and promote efficiency, the peak rate of import duty was reduced from 65 per cent to 50 per cent in 1995, and further down to 40 per cent in the 1997-98 budget.

2.3.3 Import Tariff Rationalisation: Developments

A special customs duty of 2 per cent was imposed in the 1996-97 budget and a further special customs duty of 3 per cent was imposed on certain items in 1997-98. In other words, special customs duty of 5 per cent was in force for a period valid till 31.3.1999. However, the Finance Minister announced in his 1999-2000 budget speech the discontinuance of the 5 per cent special customs duty with effect from 28.2.1999.

In another significant move, the Finance Minister reduced the then existing 7 major ad valorem rates of customs duty to the following 5 basic rates:

5 per cent (the existing one)

15 per cent (by substituting the existing 10 per cent rate)

25 per cent (by merging the 20 per cent and 25 per cent rates)

35 per cent (by merging the 30 per cent and 35 per cent rates)

40 per cent (the existing one)

However, in another move the Finance Minister imposed a uniform surcharge of 10 per cent on all commodities excluding the following categories:

Crude oil and petroleum products.

Items attracting 40 per cent rate of basic duty.

Certain GATT-bound items.

Gold and silver.

In other words, the imposition of surcharge raised the basic rate by 10 per cent. For example, basic rate of 5 per cent became 5.5 per cent and 15 per cent became 16.5 per cent.

Still further, the Finance Minister reduced the peak rate of basic customs duty from 40 per cent to 35 per cent in his 2000-2001 budget, thereby reducing the total number of customs duty rates from 5 to 4, i.e. 35 per cent, 25 per cent, 15 per cent and 5 per cent. The surcharge of 10 per cent imposed in the 1999-2000 budget became applicable to new peak rate of 35 per cent.

However, in the 2001-2002 budget, the surcharge of 10 per cent was discontinued, making the peak level of customs duty decline from 38.5 per cent to 35 per cent. As regards further reduction in the peak rate of duty, the Finance

Minister observed, "I have already promised that our customs tariff would be brought down to East Asian levels. I will like to move progressively within three years to reduce the number of rates to the minimum with a peak rate of 20%." [5]. It is noteworthy that apart from the basic customs duty, countervailing duty equivalent to excise duty (16 per cent) is also imposed, making the maximum rate of customs duty to around 50 per cent.

2.3.4 Export Tariff Policy

Export duties can become an important source of revenue when a country enjoys monopoly or near-monopoly in certain products in the international market. In the early 1950s, India had a foreign market dominance in commodities such as jute, tea, and textiles. Hence, export duties fetched sizeable revenues. As this dominance grew weaker over the years, the rates of export duty had to be reduced.

Although at present the share of export duties in customs revenue is negligible (0.5 per cent), it was not always so. In the early 1950s, export duties formed a significant proportion of customs revenue, though this situation could not be maintained for long. The yield from export duties reached a peak figure when it formed 29.9 per cent of total customs revenue in 1950-51. By 1960-61, export duty revenue had been reduced to 8.2 per cent of total customs revenue. Another upsurge in the relative share of export duties was observed in 1970-71 when they formed 12.0 per cent of customs revenue. Since then, their revenue importance has continuously decreased and in fact they have virtually disappeared.

Despite the fact that export duties have lost their

importance from revenue angle, they have not been completely dispensed with. Occasions do arise when there is considerable disparity between the domestic and international prices of certain goods enjoying a comparatively stronger position in the export market, and levying of export duties may be justified to mop up a part of the profits of the exporters. At present, export duties are levied on a few commodities such as coffee, mica, black pepper, hides and skins and leather. Export duty on an item is levied after considering such factors as domestic production and likely exportable surpluses, demand for the item in the foreign markets, changes in exchange rates, and the prices prevailing in the international market. It may be noted that the Government enjoys powers to impose and enhance export duties without prior approval of the Parliament on the consideration that such duties do not fall on the Indian consumers.

2.4 Conclusions

To recapitulate, radical reforms have been introduced in the Indian customs tariff between 1991 and 2001. These reforms were necessary because the customs tariff had become, over the years, very complicated in terms of multiple rates, innumerable exemptions, excessive controls, and elaborate procedures. These infirmities of the customs tariff often led to delays, harassment, corruption, and litigation. Moreover, rationalisation and simplification of the customs duties was needed to move towards a market economy, freedom of trade, and opening up the Indian economy to the outside world.

The major changes included the following: (a) the peak rate of import duty was reduced from 200 per cent to 35 per cent, (b) average rate of import duty was scaled down from 50 per cent to 25 per cent, (c) import duty on capital goods was brought down from 85 per cent to 25 per cent. The country has moved towards moderate rates of taxation with a view to improve compliance and reduce litigation. It is a positive step by India in an effort to position itself as an upcoming economic power. The liberalised approach to trade policy will enable in creating an environment of freer and more competitive market and will help India in achieving higher rate of growth and maintaining it also.

Notes

1. S., Sunanda: *'Trade and Dependence - Essays on Indian Economy'*; Sage Publications, 2000.

2. Government of India , *Economic Survey,* 1995-96, p. 110.

3. Government of India, Ministry of Finance, *Long Term Fiscal Policy,* December 1985, p. 41.

4. Government of India, Ministry of Finance, *Interim Report of Tax Reforms Committee* (Chairman: Raja Chelliah), December 1991, p. 1.

5. Government of India, Ministry of Finance, *Budget Speech of the Finance Minister, 2001-2002, Part B,* p. 31.

Chapter 3

India's Foreign Trade, 1991-2001: An Analysis

3.1 Introduction

India's foreign trade shares in the ups and downs of the economic growth and development of the country. The country's trade and balance of payments deficit has become a structural feature of the economy, which calls for varied policy instruments to promote production and investment and to treat equally both exports promotion and imports substitution. Against this background, an attempt has been made to see the trends in India's foreign trade during the last fifty years and the steps to be taken in future to further improve it. Export promotion and import restrictions have been the main plank of our trade policies. It was only from the mid-seventies or in particular the late seventies, that foreign trade had come to mean exports and imports.

The developmental rate of exports and imports - in particular that of the latter had been recognised, and import management rather than import restrictions was entering as a specific feature of the policy frame. India's foreign trade with her trading partners has not only grown at differential rates but has also determined by different forces, some of which have been common to all regions and countries and others have been unique to particular regions. One of the common factors have been the structural changes which have occurred in the Indian economy and have taken her far in the way of economic development and made her capable of offering various manufactured goods and more of value-added items which were previously absent in her export basket.

At present, India's exports by major commodity goods are: (a) Manufactures which include Engineering goods, Chemicals and Allied products, Cotton yarn, fabrics etc., Jute manufactures, Leather and its manufactures, Readymade garments, gems and jewellery, Together, they accounted for 81.6 per cent in 1999-2000.

(b) Agriculture and allied products category includes cashew kernels, coffee, marine products, Raw cotton, Rice, Spices, Sugar, Tea and Mate, Tobacco, etc. Together these accounted for 14.6 per cent of total exports in 1999-2000.

3.2 Export-Import Performance During 1991-2001

Since the inception of the planning era, India's foreign trade has made new strides in different directions. New markets have been explored, new items have been added to the export-basket and traditional commodities like tea, leather, jute manufacturers, etc. have been marketed with more value added to them. More stress has been placed by the government on software exports which is considered one of the booming industry keeping in view the immense human potential India has.

On the import front, developmental imports have predominated accompanied by phases of import curbs and controls as well as liberalisation. These changes had taken place parallel to economic development more often as a prerequisite arising out of the needs and priorities of the economy moulded through different Governmental policies and other factors such as economic,social and political conditions prevailing in domestic economy and rest of the world. As a result, there emerged the spatial structure of India's trade with rest of the world which is not the same in pattern which had existed at the beginning of the planning period.

3.3 Trends in Exports During 1991-2001

Trends in India' exports during the post-liberalisation period are now discussed.

3.3.1 Agricultural and Allied Goods

In early nineties, i.e. 1990-91, agricultural and allied goods exported were valued at Rs. 6,317 crore but there was a tremendous fall in their share to 19.40 per cent. In 1994-95, Rs. 13,712 crore worth of agricultural and allied goods were exported with a share of 16 per cent in the total exports of our country. The year 1996-97, however, saw an increase in the share of agricultural goods, which was 20.3 per cent but fell down a little to 18.8 per cent in 1997-98 with export figures standing at Rs. 24239 crore and 25419 crore respectively.

Share of agricultural and allied goods stood at 18.1 per cent in 1998-99 and have dropped considerably to 14.6 per cent in 1999-2000 with figures standing at Rs. 26104 crore and Rs. 24576 crore respectively. Provisional figures show that the share is expected to be around 12.2 for the period April-October 2000-2001.

In 1990-91, after a gap of 10 years, there was still not much rise in the export of coffee, as Rs. 252 crore worth of it was exported. In 1994-95, however, there was a sharp increase in the export of coffee, its value being Rs. 1053 crore showing an increase of 318 per cent over 1990-91. In 1997-98, coffee exports further rose to Rs. 1696 crore, accounting for 1.3 per cent of India's total exports. The coffee exports stood at Rs. 1364 crore in 1999-2000, a sharp decline of -9.0 per cent over the previous year.

Tea has been the most important traditional commodity in our exports. The Indian tea industry is a prolific source of foreign exchange for the Central and State Governments.

Exports of tea declined a little to Rs. 975 crore in 1994-95 rising again to Rs. 1171 crore in 1995-96. In 1997-98, tea exported by our country was valued at Rs. 1,505 crore which depicted a rise of 45 per cent over 1996-97. Beginning of nineties saw a further fall in its share which was just 3.28 per cent in 1990-91.

In 1994-95, it registered a decrease again to 1.2 per cent only. From mid-nineties, however, share of tea has been more or less constant (changing to 0.8 per cent only in 1996-97) at 1.2 per cent. In 1998-99, share of tea in our total exports was 1.09 per cent amounting to Rs. 2265 crore and stood at 1766 crore in 1999-2000, a sharp fall of (-)24.3 per cent.

The beginning of nineties saw a drastic fall in the share of tobacco in total goods exported by India. It declined to 0.81 per cent in 1990-91. In 1994-95, it further came down to 0.2 per cent. In 1997-98 its share was 0.80 per cent. UK had been the most important market for India in the 1950's, but at present it is exported mainly to Belgium, Germany, the Netherlands, Japan and Singapore. For the year 1999-2000, tobacco exports stood at Rs. 993 crore.

3.3.2 Manufactured Goods

This is a major commodity group exported by India, whose share in the total exports of our country has consistently grown from 1950-51 till date. In 1990-91, there was a sharp increase in the share of this commodity group, it represented 72.90 per cent of the total exports by India. In 1994-95, its share further rose to 78.1 per cent. It declined a little to 74.1 per cent in 1996-97 and in 1998-99, its share was 77.7 per cent. Its share rose to 81.6 per cent in 1999-2000 with total exports at Rs. 126329 crore. The share is however, expected to decline marginally to 80.6 per cent for the year 2000-2001.

The consistent rise in the share of this commodity group can be attributed to many major commodities, whose exports have shown a remarkable increase in a span of 50 years. These goods include gems and jewellery, ready-made garments, cotton yarn and fabrics, leather and leather manufactures, machinery and electronic goods etc.

In 1995-96, foreign exchange earnings received through this commodity reached a peak of Rs. 8619 crore showing a rise of 310.4 per cent over 1990-91. In 1997-98, cotton yarn exported was valued at Rs. 12,094 crore.

Exports of ready-made garments increased to Rs. 4012 crore in 1990-91 registering a growth rate of 629 per cent over the previous decade. In 1995-96, Rs. 12295 crore worth of ready-made garments were exported showing a growth of 206 per cent over 1990-91. In 1997-98, Rs. 14032 crore worth of garments were exported, showing a marginal rise of 14 per cent over mid-nineties. In 1998-99 and 1999-2000, ready-made garments had a share of 13.1 per cent and 12.8 per cent respectively. The figures for 1999-2000 stood at Rs. 20809 crore.

In 1990-91, foreign exchange earnings through the export of leather and its manufactures was Rs. 2600 crore which registered a growth of 566.66 per cent over 1980-81. In mid-nineties, i.e. 1995-96, the value of leather goods exported doubled to Rs. 5,790 crore. In 1997-98, there was a marginal decline in the export of this value, it came down to Rs. 5,461 crore. In 1997-98 and 1998-99, leather and its manufactures including footwear had a share of 4.3 per cent and 4.18 per cent respectively. However, this share has declined in 1999-2000 hovering at 3.4.

In 1990-91 the value of gems and jewellery exported was Rs. 5247 crore registering a growth of 749 per cent over its previous decade. In 1995-96, gems and jewellery exported were valued at Rs. 17644 crore which depicted a rise of 236 per cent over its value in 1990-91. In 1997-98, gems and jewellery rose only by 8 per cent over its value in 1995-96, the value being Rs. 19,014 crore.

During 1999-2000, this commodity generated an export figure of Rs. 33089 crore and is expected to have a share of 18.0 per cent in 2000-2001.

In 1990-91, foreign exchange earnings from machinery and electronic goods were valued at Rs. 3872 crore, showing a tremendous rise by 368 per cent over 1980-81. In mid-nineties, i.e. 1995-96 Rs. 14,578 crore worth of these goods were exported which showed a rise of 276.4 per cent over 1990-91.

In 1997-98, foreign exchange earned from the export of these goods were valued at Rs. 18,354 crore showing a marginal rise of 26 per cent over 1995-96.

In 1999-2000, the share of this commodity stood at 4.6 per cent with total value at Rs. 21435 crore.

The composition of exports reveals a gradual shift during the nineties. The share of ores and minerals has declined progressively from 4.6 per cent in 1991-92 to 2.4 per cent in 1999-2000 with an expected share of 2.7 for the current year.

The share of manufactured goods, the dominant sector,

has been fluctuating around 80 per cent. The share of agricultural and allied goods has been more variable, declining from 1991-92 to 1994-95, rising during the subsequent two years and dropping again since 1997-98. This is, in part, due to lack of a consistent agricultural export policy and frequent supply considerations restraining aggressive trade promotion of these exports.

As per *Economic Survey, 2000-2001*, for the period April-October of the current financial year, share of agricultural and allied goods is expected to be 12.2 per cent, a decline of almost 3 per cent compared to corresponding period last year.

Share of Ores and minerals is expected to be stagnant hovering around 2.4 per cent mark. manufactured goods share is expected to decline marginally at would be pegged at around 80 per cent of India's total exports. The trends in Indian exports of major items from 1990-91 to 2000-2001 is presented in Table 3.1.

India's share in world exports has been less than 1 per cent during a period of 50 years (1950-51 to 2000-2001). However, an interesting and encouraging feature to note is that India commands an important place in world trade in tea, rice, precious and semi-precious stones, spices, coffee, leather and its manufactures, and iron-ore.

In 1996, the share of India in world trade in the following commodities was as shown in the parentheses: Rice (12.0 per cent), Tea and mate (11.1 per cent), Spices (11.2 per cent), Iron-ore (7.8 per cent), manufactures of leather (6.2 per cent), precious and semi-precious stones (10.8 per cent).

Table 3.1: India's Major Export Items (1990-91 to 2000-2001)

(in Rs. crore)

Comodity Group	1990-91	1995-96	1997-98	1998-99	1999-2000	2000-2001*
1. Agricultural & Allied Products	6317	21138	25419	26104	24576	25500
2. Ores & Minerals	1497	3061	3062	2827	2975	4150
3. Manufacured Goods	23736	80219	99824	109787	126329	132023
4. Mineral Fuels & Lubricants	948	1761	1399	594	467	--
5. Others						
TOTAL	**32553**	**106353**	**130101**	**139753**	**162925**	**165186**

* Projections

Source: 1. *Economic Survey, 2000-2001*, Government of India, New Delhi; 2. CMIE, *Monthly Review of the Indian Economy, May 2001*; 3. DGCI&S, (October 2000 issue).

3.4 Trends in Imports during 1991-2001

India's major imports are petroleum oil and lubricants, capital goods, pearls and precious stones, fertilisers, iron and steel, chemicals and edible oils. Together they accounted for nearly 70 per cent in 1997-98 of total goods. In the year 1999-2000, the above mentioned items accounted for about 63.2 per cent of the total imports.

In 1990-91, the value of POL imported double to Rs. 10816 crore. In 1995-96 and 1997-98, imports reached a figure of Rs. 25173 crore and Rs. 30538 crore respectively. In the year 1998-99 and 1999-2000, their total value stood at Rs. 26, 919 and Rs. 45421 crore respectively. In 1990-91, share of POL dropped to 25.04 per cent and further to 20.5 per cent in 1995-96. In 1997-98 and 1998-99, its share has been 20.2 per cent and 15.1 per cent respectively. The share stood at 22.2 per cent in 1999-2000 and is expected to be 21.0 per cent as per *Economic Survey, 2000-2001*.

In 1990-91, chemicals imported were valued at Rs. 2298 crore which indicated a growth rate of 539.3 per cent over 1980-81. In 1995-96 and 1997-98 chemicals imported were worth Rs. 9403 crore and Rs. 12128 crore respectively.

In 1996-97, chemicals had a large share 7.50 per cent in the total imports of our country and which marginally increased to 8.0 per cent in 1997-98. In 1998-99, chemicals had a share of 0.70 per cent. The share of total chemicals imported in 1999-2000 was 8.3 per cent, a marginal decrease of 0.5 per cent over the previous year.

In 1990-91, capital goods imported were valued at Rs. 10466 crore, rising by 447.9 per cent over 1980-81. In 1995-96, Rs. 28289 crore worth of capital goods were imported which decreased a little to Rs. 26532 crore in 1997-98, declining by 6.15 per cent. The share of capital goods declined slightly to 23.05 per cent in 1995-96. In 1997-98, capital goods had a share of 17.5 per cent in the total imports of our country and in 1998-99, this share rose to 18.1 per cent. However, in the year 1999-2000, the total value of capital goods imported was pegged at Rs. 23999 crore, a substantial decline to 11.4 per cent share.

The above analysis shows that the structure of our imports has undergone a great change in recent years. The desire for rapid industrialisation necessitated large imports of machinery, capital goods, transport equipment and project goods. While earlier manufactured commodities predominated in our imports, over a period of few decades petroleum, oil and lubricants and capital goods have dominated our imports.

In recent years, there has been significant reduction in the imports of cereal and cereal products, fertilisers and metals besides many other goods with the progress of import substitution and higher production in the country.

In the composition of imports in the recent past reveals a rising share of food and allied products from 3.6 per cent in 1996-97 to 5.6 per cent in 1999-2000 and is expected to further rise to 7.1 per cent in the current year. The share of POL in total imports has declined from 25.65 per cent in 1996-97 to 22.2 per cent in 1999-2000, mainly due to low international crude oil prices and is expected to further decline to 21 per cent in 2000-2001 mainly because of low diesel off take in the first quarter.

Similarly, capital goods share in total imports declined from 21.5 per cent in 1996-97 to 11.4 per cent in 1999-2000, on account of reduced imports of transport equipment, machinery (except electrical) and machine tools.

Similarly, the share of other imports has also decreased

from 35.4 per cent in 1998-99 to 33.8 per cent in 1999-2000 and is expected to register a sharp decline to 28.7 per cent, mainly due to a sharp decrease in imports of gold and silver.

Other commodities whose imports recorded significant growth in 1999-2000 were: fuel (24.3 per cent), fertilisers (2.9 per cent), and unclassified items (21.0 per cent) as per Economic Survey, 2000-2001.

3.5 Regional Groupings

The post-war world has been marked by the emergence of various trade blocs. The concept of a trade block can be best described as a group of countries coming together and allowing, within the group, complete freedom in the movement of goods, capital and services. Interestingly, West Europe, went a step further by announcing that in their 1992 programme, there would not only be complete freedom in the movement of goods, capital and services, but also people, thus popularising the term Four Freedoms.

This on-going trend of block formation is a very dynamic process and inevitably leads to deeper and wider integration. A classic example is of the development of the European Integration process which has progressed in leaps and bounds, since the establishment of European Coal and Steel Community (ECSC) in 1948. Since then, this Western European trade block moved to the establishment of European Union in 1994 and is now aspiring to establish the European Monetary System (EMS) by the first decade of the next century. Furthermore, this union started as a block of only six nations but now is a formidable block of fifteen; with further eastward expansion being a distinct possibility.

The direction of India's trade gives a picture of both the destination of exports and the origin of imports from 1990-

91 to 2000-2001.

From the analysis, it is imperative that EU as in 1999-2000 was India's largest trading partner accounting for 25.71 per cent of its total exports to the world. USA emerged as the second largest trading partner accounting for 22.85 per cent of India's exports to the world followed by OPEC and Japan which had a share of 11.21 per cent and 4.61 per cent respectively in 1999-2000. Asia is also one of the largest trading partners of our country and had accounted for 24.89 per cent of India's exports to the world in 1999-2000.

Regarding, percentage share of India's major trading partners (imports), EU accounted for 22.75 per cent of India's total imports from the world in 1999-2000. OPEC countries also accounted for 17.95 per cent of India's total imports from the world in 1999-2000. Asia accounted for almost 24.50 per cent of India's imports from the world followed by USA and Japan which had a share of 7.91 per cent and 4.86 per cent of India's imports from the world respectively in 1999-2000. A detailed analysis of these important trading partners is given below.

3.5.1 India-EU Trade Relations

Indo-EU economic relationship is now more than three and a half decades old. India's relationship with the Union has always been marked by mutual co-operation and trust. India's exports to EU can be classified into following broad categories:

- Agricultural and Marine products;
- Leather and its products including Footwear.
- Chemicals and allied products.
- Textiles and Garments.
- Jute and Coir products.

- Gems and Jewellery.
- Engineering and Electronic goods.

Nearly 70 per cent of India's exports to EU comprise of commodities which include leather, tea, diamonds, cotton fabrics, tobacco, precious and semi-precious stones and coffee.

The residual exports of about 30 per cent comprising engineering goods, chemicals and software form a dynamic area which still has a wider scope for exploitation. A look at the figures reveals that from 1973-74 to 1999-2000, major partners have been U.K., Germany, Belgium, Italy, the Netherlands and France. In the 1970s, i.e. from 1973-74 to 1979-80, U.K. dominated the European Union by having a share of 29 per cent (maximum share of 46.60 per cent in 1975-76).

From 1995-96 onwards, share of U.K. in India's total exports to EU started rising and that of Germany started declining. As in 1999-2000, U.K. is the leading trade partner followed closely by Germany. A notable feature from 1993-94 onwards is that Belgium has become an important trade partner, its rank being third in 1999-2001 with per cent exports of 3.70 and is expected to retain the same position in the current year.

Greece, Luxembourg, Portugal, Denmark, Ireland and Spain are small partners. Share of Luxembourg till 1992-93 had almost been negligible. Share of Portugal, Greece, Ireland was even less than 1 per cent of India's total exports to EU. In 1997-98, these countries together accounted for 9.95 per cent of total exports to EU, showing a remarkable increase from 1992-93. Share of Spain has however, fallen from 1.98 per cent in 1983-84 to 1.53 per cent in 1999-2000.

India imports almost 1/3rd of its total imports from

European Union.

Share of India's imports from EU fell in the early 1990s; in 1993-94, its share was 30 per cent. It however, started declining from 1994-95 and as in 1999-2000, its share was 22.75 per cent and is expected to further decline to 20.40 per cent in 2000-2001.

India's imports from EU cover a wide range of items like

- Iron and Steel
- Gems and Jewellery, particularly rough diamonds.
- Capital goods, particularly machinery and transport equipment.
- Organic chemicals.
- Inorganic chemicals.
- Chemical material and products.
- Non-ferrous metals.
- Professional and Scientific instruments etc.

Together, they accounted for 74.55 per cent of total imports in 1997-98.

Within EU, in 1997-98, major import sources were U.K. (21 per cent), Germany (19 per cent), Belgium (11 per cent) followed by Italy (8 per cent) and France (7.5 per cent). Share of U.K. fell from 34 per cent in 1973-74 to 21 per cent in 1997-98. Belgium has emerged as the most important source for imports as its share has risen from 9 per cent in 1973-74 to 12 per cent in 1997-98. Thus, imports from EU are highly concentrated in countries like Germany, U.K., France, Italy and Belgium.

3.5.1.1 United Kingdom: From 1995-96 onwards, UK is the number one trading partner with India. India's major exports to UK included Ready-made garments (11 per cent), Leather (7 per cent), gems and Jewellery (6 per cent), Engineering goods (6 per cent).

Exports in 1990-91 to U.K. amounted to Rs. 2128 crore (23.77 per cent of total exports to EU) as compared to exports to Germany which amounted to Rs. 2549 crore with 28.47 per cent share.

It is evident that U.K.'s share of tea and mate in India's total exports of it to world is the highest (13 per cent in 1997-98). India's exports of tobacco etc. to world in 1997-98 was Rs. 1058.51 crore and U.K.'s share was Rs. 138.12 crore representing a share of 13 per cent.

3.5.1.2 Germany: Germany is not only the largest market for Indian exports but also the most important source of imports for India among all the EU member countries, sharing 22 per cent of total exports and 20 per cent of total imports in 1997-98.

India's major exports to Germany include Ready-made garments, Leather and its manufactures, Carpets and other floor coverings.

After the unification in 1990, exports increased from Rs. 2548 crore in 1990-91 to Rs. 7155 crore in 1997-98 registering a growth of 170 per cent and further to Rs. 7809 crore in 1999-2000.

Major imports from Germany include capital goods, especially electrical and non-electrical machinery, Iron and Steel, Organic chemicals and Chemical material and products.

India's imports from Germany stood at Rs. 3473 in 1990-91, registering an increase of 16.6 per cent over the previous year. During the period from 1980-81 to 1989-90, India's imports from the then West Germany increased by 325 per cent . The exports during this period increased by 361 per cent . They grew faster than the imports.

In the early 90s, i.e., 1990-91 to 1992-93, India had

witnessed a constant fall in the balance of trade with Germany. Germany has also emerged as India's leading source for foreign technology and foreign direct investment.

In the early 90s, i.e., 1991-92, Germany had maximum number of foreign collaborations approved and had second position in the country-wise foreign investments in India; Germany accounted for 35 per cent of the total foreign investments approved in India from 1991 to 1994.

Despite increases in volume and value in the bilateral trade, from the Indian point of view, the share of Indo-German trade in Germany's aggregate trade has been very small, being merely about 0.5 per cent of the total German trade volume in the last years of the 1990s. German imports from India constitute only a minuscule of its total imports (around 0.3 per cent) and German supplies, in terms of its world-wide exports, also form a very negligible portion (about 0.5 per cent).

3.5.2 India's Trade with USA

With the erosion of India's traditional bonds with the sterling era since the middle of the fifties, trade with the United States of America, especially imports, came into prominence, attained great heights in the sixties and then gradually fell over the years as proportion of India's total trade. India's dependence on USA grew in terms of critical imports like foodgrains, fertilisers and capital goods, in terms of the aid that it provided and the technology which it exported.

The US involvement in India's economic development, accounting for the aid-relationship which India had with US since 1952, enhanced trade rapidly especially imports - a concomitant outcome of tied-aid that climbed to massive proportions in the fifties and continued through the sixties.

However, the heights gained by the USA in India's trade was short lived. During the middle and late sixties, the US Government along with the World Bank subjected the Indian economy to strict standards of performance using the non-project (or programme) loans as levers for exhorting such standards. Reforms advocated by the donors such as greater agricultural priority, new agricultural strategy, liberalisation of trade and correction of an over-valued exchange rate led to the devaluation of the Indian rupee in June, 1966 and liberalisation of imports (in expectation of a substantial rise in the level of non-project loans). But, the much expected increment in aid did not take place and the adverse domestic reactions to such pressures virtually amounting to US intrusion were enormous.

Economic assistance was further cut in the early seventies which had an adverse impact on , development efforts. Again, the Indo-US relationship was further strained in 1971 by US's tilt towards Pakistan, and later with its involvement in the Indian ocean.

An attempt has been made to analyse India's trade with USA over the period 1950-51 to 1999-2000 with focus specially on the last decade. On the average, exports to USA had been nearly 20 per cent of India's exports over 1950-75 which fell to an average of 14 per cent over 1976-82 but subsequently increased to 19 per cent during 1983-85. Imports had fluctuated over the time period studied but hovered around 30 per cent, approximately of India's total imports during 1950-75 which declined to an average of 16 per cent after mid-seventies.

3.5.2.1 Exports: USA covers more than 80 per cent, on an average, of India's exports to the dollar area and is also a major importer of India's total exports. At the initial stages of planned development, India having mainly traditional goods to offer, the principal items of exports were jute manufactures, tea, spices, cashew kernels, cotton textiles, metal ores, minerals etc. Jute manufactures accounted for the highest proportion of exports to USA in 1950-51, followed by spices, their respective shares being 30.5 per cent and 13.3 per cent of India's total exports to USA.

The pattern of trade with USA underwent gradual changes, over the time period studied and the traditional items of exports dwindled in importance yielding place to a variety of non-traditional products such as precious stones, works of art, floor coverings etc. whose proportion in total exports to USA increased over the years. To deal with the sophisticated market as that of USA, changes in the composition of trade were essential. Hence, new products, manufactured and semi-manufactured such as jewellery, handicrafts, food products, footwear, engineering goods etc., made for gradual diversification of exports. Further, the share of consumer goods in total US import basket showed a secular tendency to decline. This also affected unfavourably India's consumer goods imports to US in the long run.

In the seventies, mineral fuel and industrial raw materials gained increasing shares of total imports by US whereby India's exports basket become structurally much different from that of US import basket. Export of jute manufactures suffered a severe setback with the share falling from 30.5 per cent in 1950-51 to 4.6 per cent in 1981-82. The share of jute fell further down to 1.04 per cent, 0.28 per cent, 0.36 per cent and 0.35 per cent in 1991-92, 1992-93, 1993-94 and 1994-95 respectively. Two factors were responsible for this: one, East Pakistan (now Bangladesh since 1971) from 1958 provided stiff competition to India in the international field, and two, the use of jute as a packaging material tended to decline due to the method of bulk-handling and due to emergence of substitutes, such as polypropylene as a substitute for hurlap and use of paper bags.

The relative share of tea in India's exports to USA, similarly went down to 0.6 per cent in 1981-82 from 7.9 per cent in 1950-51, due to Sri Lanka, East Africa and Indonesia having emerged as India's main competitors, and because the high price of Indian tea acted as a negative incentive with regard to its exports. Coffee provided a strong substitute whose proportion in India's total exports to USA increased.

As for mica, exports to USA declined from 6.7 per cent in 1950-51 to a negligible proportion in 1993-94 because of declining consumption of sheet mica in USA, following the expanding and extensive use of synthetics. The uncompetitive prices offered by India was a contributory factor.

Relative share of spices, raw hides and skins, lac etc. also declined in total exports to USA; whereas that of floor coverings, precious and semi-precious stones and clothing reached 4.7 per cent, 26.1 per cent and 14.4 per cent respectively by the end of 1981-82. Together, these non-traditional items constituted more than 40 per cent of total exports to USA in 1981-82 and 48.49 per cent in 1991-92 and 50.05 per cent in 1993-94. In 1997-98 and 1998-99, their share together was 50 per cent and 54 per cent respectively. Agricultural and allied products also constitute an important source of foreign exchange from USA. Their share was 9.57 per cent and 9.21 per cent respectively in 1997-98 and 1998-99. Among this group, cashew and spices from an important source accounting for 2.32 per cent and

1.67 per cent in 1998-99.

The devaluation of the rupee which took place on June 6, 1966 and the new duties imposed on India's major traditional exportables had cast their unfavourable impact on trade with the dollar area because India had mainly traditional goods to offer to USA which had low price elasticities.

Another reason for slow growth in trade between India and USA till 1980s was that USA being a developed country with a highly sophisticated market, changes in taste and technology so frequently that a developing country like India with limited resources at its disposal and with relatively inelastic infrastructure of production found it difficult to keep pace with it.

From 1990's trade with USA improved substantially. From a share of 14.7 per cent in 1990-91 in India's total exports to world, USA's share increased to 19.1 per cent in 1994-95 and 19.5 per cent in 1997-98. In 1998-99, USA accounted for 21.78 per cent share of total goods exported by India to the world and in 1999-2000 its share stood at 22.7 per cent and is expected to decline marginally to 21.56 per cent in 2000-2001.

3.5.2.2 Imports: Imports from USA played a crucial role in India's foreign trade in the fifties, as well as in the sixties. Imports of foodgrains, fertilisers and capital equipment from dollar area, gave a major thrust in increasing the trade deficit in the period mentioned above.

By the beginning of the seventies, the urgency of food, fertilisers and capital goods imports lessened except for the world food crisis, in the first half of the 1970's when India's food imports from USA amounted to Rs. 894.8 crore and Rs. 606.1 crore in 1975-76 and 1976-77 respectively which dropped to Rs. 432 crore only by the end of 1998-99. Oil imports gradually gained grounds consequent upon the spate of increase in oil prices by OPEC.

In 1950-51, the share of foodgrains, fertilisers and capital equipment was 14.5 per cent, 3.4 per cent and 13.1 per cent respectively which was 42.8 per cent, 4.0 per cent and 19.3 per cent in 1960-61 respectively. In 1970-71 and 1981-82, however, their shares were 29.3 per cent, 4.0 per cent and 33.7 per cent and 17.4 per cent, 18.6 per cent and 30.6 per cent respectively.

In 1991-92 and 1993-94, the share of foodgrains fertilisers and capital equipment was 1.21 per cent, 15.5 per cent, and 26.47 per cent and 1.03 per cent, 5.91 per cent and 54.72 per cent respectively. In 1997-98 and 1998-99, the share of foodgrains, fertilisers and capital equipment was 3.04 per cent, 6 per cent and 36 per cent and 2.82 per cent, 7 per cent and 31 per cent respectively.

The main items imported from the United States include transport equipment, machinery except electrical and machine tools, project goods, electrical machinery, fertilisers manufactured, organic chemicals, chemical material and products, pearls, precious and semi-precious stones etc. Together these accounted for 61 per cent in 1998-99.

USA is an important destination for Indian exports and an equally important source of imports. From a share of 16 per cent in India's total exports to world in 1960-61, its share has grown to 22.7 per cent in 1999-2000.

As far as imports are concerned, USA accounted for 29 per cent in 1960-61 of total Indian imports from the world, but its share fell to 7.7 per cent in 1999-2000 and is expected to further fall to 5.5 per cent in 2000-2001. More efforts are required to improve the share of goods exported to USA.

3.5.3 India's Trade with OPEC

The thirteen oil-exporting developing countries which constitute the OPEC attracted a great deal of attention in the seventies by their sudden move to increase oil prices in 1973-74 and raising it still further subsequently in 1979-80. Benchmark prices of crude petroleum rose dramatically by nearly 82 per cent between 1970 and 1973 and again by more than 250 per cent between 1973 and 1974. Further, oil prices rose once again by 83 per cent in 1979-80 after falling by 9 per cent between 1975 and 1978 in real terms.

While the balance of trade and payments position of the oil-exporting countries improved markedly on account of increased inflow of surplus earnings on oil exports, the rest of the world consisting of both developed and developing countries was thrown into a total disarray. Increased oil prices shot up the prices of fertilisers which had an adverse impact on agricultural production. In the Industrial sector too, such prices had a depressing effect on oil-based industries such as automobiles, petrochemicals etc. Costs of production increased with output shrinking and there was a general world inflation with increase in cost of living.

Although, India was amongst a few developing countries who could locate huge domestic reserves of oil and natural gas her immediate import requirements of oil could not be cut down to any appreciable extent and OPEC emerged as a major trading partner of India in relation to imports, claiming nearly one-fourth of India's total imports in the seventies.

Of the goods exported, tea, jute manufactures cotton textiles and spices made up for 17 per cent, 10 per cent, 17 per cent and 3 per cent, respectively of India's total exports to OPEC. On imports sides, oil imports accounted for nearly

80 per cent of total imports. The balance of trade was, in general, surplus for India.

In the process of export diversification, few more commodities like engineering items and handicrafts were added to India's export list but imported items remained more or less the same from these countries.

Nineties have proved to be very important for India's foreign trade with OPEC. Our trade with OPEC has improved substantially and OPEC's share in Indian exports has increased from 5.6 per cent in 1990-91 to 10.6 per cent in 1999-2000. Share of imports from OPEC have risen from 16 per cent in 1990-91 to 24 per cent in 1999-2000. Major goods exported to OPEC in 1998-99 included agricultural products (31 per cent), chemicals (8.2 per cent), engineering goods (17 per cent), RMG (14 per cent). Goods imported from OPEC include capital goods as well as material and intermediaries.

3.5.4 India's Trade with Japan

Japan has been an important trading partner of India since fifties. India's exports to Japan accounted for 5.5 per cent in 1960-61 and share of imports was 5.4 per cent in the same year.

In, 1990-91, share of exports to Japan was 9.3 per cent whereas imports had a share of 7.5 per cent. In mid-nineties, exports to Japan had a share of 7.7 per cent and imports from Japan also had a share of 7.1 per cent. In 1999-2000, the share of exports and imports from Japan fell down to 4.5 per cent and 5.0 per cent respectively.

In 1950-51, seeds were the major exports, claiming a share of nearly 48.8 per cent. Ores of iron and manganese had a share of more than 11 per cent of total exports. This structure changed in the sixties when export of seeds receded to the background. In 1960-61, iron-ore and its concentrates and raw cotton accounted for 63.6 per cent of India's exports to Japan.

By 1970-71, the market for raw cotton exports was substituted partly by iron ore and its concentrates, iron and steel and fish exports. Export of fish and fish preparation from India entered the Japanese market in a big way.

In 1990s, principal commodities exported by India to Japan included gems and jewellery, marine products, RMG cotton including accessories, ores and minerals, cashew, carpet (excluding silk) etc. Together these accounted for more than 60 per cent share in total exports to Japan in 1998-99.

In the 1990s, major items imported from Japan included machinery except electrical and machine tools; project goods, iron and steel, transport equipment, organic chemicals, etc.

India had a deficit of Rs. 5 crore and Rs. 6 crore in 1950-51 and 1960-61 respectively. However, there was a trade surplus of Rs. 121 crore in 1970-71. But in eighties again we had a trade deficit of Rs. 200 crore. In 1990-91 too, we had a similar trade deficit of Rs. 206 crore which increased to Rs. 3087 crore in 1998-99.

3.6 Conclusion

Exports have on the whole showed a significant recovery in 1999-2000 from the negative growth experienced in 1998-99. The current account deficit has been contained at 0.9 per cent of GDP despite substantial increase in oil import bill by 63 per cent following hardening of international crude prices.

Export growth has been robust even in 2000-2001 because of Rupee depreciation alongwith tariff reductions, openness to foreign investment in information technology etc. As per *Economic Survey 2000-2001*, exports are expected to remain buoyant, evident from the growth rate of 20.4 per cent (in US dollar value).

India's foreign trade with her trading partners has not only grown at differential rates but has also been determined by different forces, some of which have been common to all recommendations regions and countries and others have been unique to particular regions. One of the common factors have been the structural changes which have occurred in the Indian economy and have taken her far in the way of economic development and made her capable of offering various manufactured goods and more of value-added items which were previously absent in her export basket.

India's import requirements have also changed along with the structural changes and have grown in volume too with different phases of import liberalisation at the official level since the year 1966-67. The other common factor has been the growing protectionist tendency of both developed and developing world which has adversely affected the growth of India's exports.

Quotas, tariffs, arbitrary customs valuation etc. have arrested the growth of exports to different directions in a sizeable manner. Another factor underlying directional change of trade has been the effort made at economic development by the newly developing countries which remained untapped but nevertheless, provided a vast potential market for India's trade opportunities. A negative force common to developing countries, operating on India's exports has been that of foreign exchange shortage and payment difficulties which these countries have experienced frequently and which in its turn has been a major hindrance in growth of India's exports to such countries.

Foreign competition, emergence of near-substitutes and preferential treatment granted to certain countries or certain groups of countries have also influenced direction of India's foreign trade. Trade with EU and US have been particularly affected by India's uncompetitive prices of many primary exportables which have been partially replaced from other markets as well as by close substitutes.

EU's preferential treatment for associate countries or African, Caribbean or Pacific (ACP) countries under the Lome Conventions and imposition of quotas and tariffs have also made matters difficult for Indian exports. India's exports have improved since seventies in relation to earlier decades but the growth in exports has not matched the growth in imports. There is ample scope to raise exports further. Opportunities for export growth may be located in those trade regions with whom India's trade has not registered any substantial rise as yet. Trade with countries of developing ESCAP, Latin American countries and African countries are cases in point.

India's exports have been dominated by the developed countries which have resorted to increased protectionism since the seventies and have even offered prices lower than those of other countries. Though exports cannot always flow to those countries which offer higher prices, nevertheless, it may be worthwhile to ensure that a major proportion of exports go to those countries which are in a position to give better prices. This is expected to have a beneficial impact on foreign exchange earnings.

Similarly, it would be in the interest of the country if more and more imports flow from those countries which are at relatively cheaper terms. In this manner, losses arising in trade through prices can be minimised.

Dependence on one country or partner reduces the degree of lassitude in trade transactions. Over the years, India's direction of trade has spread amongst a number of countries and regions and has not concentrated on any single country or market.

Chapter 4

India's Trade Reforms: Challenges and Strategies

4.1 Export-Import in 2000-2001: A Review

India's exports during the financial year 2000-2001 (April-March) have registered a growth of about 20 percent in dollar terms, thereby exceeding the target of 18 percent set for the year. India's exports during 2000-2001 are valued at US $ 44.1 billion, which is 19.83 percent higher than the level of US $ 36.8 billion during April-March 1999-2000. In rupee terms the exports were Rs. 201674.10 crore, which is 26.39 percent higher than the value of exports during April-March 1999-2000.

Exports during March 2001 are valued at US $ 4277.32 million which is 10.82 percent higher than the level of US $ 3859.80 million in March 2000. The value of exports in March 2001, is the highest achieved in any month in 2000-01. In rupee terms the exports were Rs. 19941.07 crore during March 2001 which is 18.53 percent higher than the value of exports during March 2000.

The main sectors that have performed well in 2000-01 are marine products, leather and leather products, basic chemicals, engineering goods, electronic goods, man-made yarn fabrics and made ups and readymade garments. India's imports during April-March 2000-01 are valued at US $ 49843.00 million representing a growth of 0.27 percent over the level of imports valued at US $ 49709.83 million in April-March 1999-2000.

Oil imports during April-March 2000-01 are valued at US $ 15653.29 million which is 62.29 percent higher than oil imports valued at US $ 9645.42 million in the corresponding period last year. Non-oil imports during April-March 2000-01 are estimated at US $ 34189.71 million which is 14.66 percent lower than the level of such imports valued at US $ 40064.41 million in April March 1999-2000.

Imports during March 2000-01 are valued at US $ 4304.02 million which is 11.65 percent lower than the level of US $ 4871.45 million in March 1999-2000. In rupee terms the imports decreased by 5.50 percent. The trade deficit for April-March 2000-01 is estimated at US $ 5739.23 million which is lower than the deficit at US $ 12904.48 million during April March 1999-2000. The good export performance has contributed to the lower trade deficit.

4.2 Trade Agenda

On the eve of the new millennium, there is a need to pause and reflect on the nation's performance particularly in the foreign trade sector and draw up a balance-sheet of achievements and shortfalls.

While our nation can take legitimate pride in the tremendous strides made on the export front over a period of 50 years, both in terms of product and market diversification, but one cannot wish away the fact that India's share in world trade continues to be a minuscule 0.6 per cent [1].

There is an imperative need for India to enlarge its share of the world trade which has been gathering increasing momentum through the cascading effect of trade reforms and the rapid integration of the world economies. The

Government of India is committed to raise India's share in world trade from the current level of 0.6 per cent to 1 per cent by the turn of the century and ultimately bring India into the major world exporters' league.

An indication of the Government's appreciation of the tasks ahead has already been demonstrated by the progressive dismantling of a large number of controls and redefining the state's role as that of a facilitator rather than a regulator of foreign trade.

Another major step in this direction has been the recent move by the Government of India to establish the Export Promotion Board which would not only improve the degree of co-ordination among the Economic Ministries of the Union Government dealing with the export sector but also be able to expedite redressal of many legitimate grievances of the exporters.

A look at Table 4.1 clearly indicates that India's share in 1950 and 1960 in world trade was 1.78 per cent and 1.36 per cent respectively. In 1970 and 1980 it decreased to 0.65 per cent and 0.57 per cent respectively. In 1997 and 1998, it further decreased to 0.62.

India had not taken any export promotion measures during late forties and the entire fifties. During early sixties and in the subsequent years, a number of measures were taken to promote exports. In spite of such special export promotion measures, our share in world trade could never cross 1 percentage point in all the subsequent years. This fact warrants an element of introspection.

4.3 Export Promotion Initiatives

It must be noted that export promotion cannot be the responsibility of the Government alone. The trade and industry must effectively participate in this movement. The Central Government has set up Export Promotion Councils, Commodity Boards and Product Oriented Development Authorities in different sectors of the foreign trade. Trading corporations, Minerals and Metals Trading Corporation and Handicrafts and Handlooms Export Corporation have also been set up to look after and transact actual export business.

Table 4.1: India's Share in World Trade: 1950-98

Select Years	India's share in world exports (%)	India's share in world imports (%)	India's share in world trade (%)
1950	1.85	1.71	1.78
1960	1.03	1.69	1.36
1970	0.64	0.65	0.65
1980	0.42	0.72	0.57
1990	0.52	0.66	0.59
1991	0.50	0.56	0.53
1992	0.53	0.61	0.57
1993	0.58	0.60	0.59
1994	0.60	0.63	0.61
1995	0.60	0.61	0.60
1996	0.62	0.63	0.62
1997	0.62	0.62	0.62
1998	0.61	0.63	0.62

Source: *1998 International Trade Statistics Yearbook:* UN,1999.

A large number of institutions including the Indian Institute of Foreign Trade, Federation of Indian Export Organisations, the Indian Institute of Packaging, the Indian

Council of Arbitration, Export Inspection Council of India etc. have been set up to impart training, pursue research and provide consultancy work relating to exports. For organising trade fairs and exhibitions within the country and abroad, the India Trade Promotion Organisation has been set up.

At the level of industry, there are apex chambers such as Associated Chamber of Commerce and Industry, Confederation of Indian Industry and Federation of Indian Chamber of Commerce and Industry. There are chambers of commerce and associations of industries in a number of states.

The present time is opportune when the working of all Institutions and Agencies connected with the exports promotion efforts need to be looked into in greater details so that they are sufficiently enthused and energised to enter the new millennium of intensified global challenges, with renewed confidence. Care should be taken to ensure that there is no overlapping and duplication of functions so that export promotion measures become more focused.

4.3.1 Infrastructural Facilities

The basic problem of Indian exports, as also of other sectors of the economy, is a lack of required infrastructural facilities. Port facilities, shipping facilities, roads, railways etc. are inadequate. All these sectors require huge investments. A proactive liberalised FDI regime has attracted a substantial amount of foreign investment in the infrastructural sector. However, the inflows, though substantial, are still insufficient to the needs. More foreign investment is needed in this direction and the Government is taking appropriate steps to improve these facilities.

4.3.2 Exploring New Markets

India can no longer depend only on its traditional trading partners. There is a need to diversify by penetrating new markets. To start with, India should concentrate on certain key markets like European Union, USA, Japan etc. so that the promotional efforts can get focused.

The Ministry of Commerce had sometimes back developed a Country-Commodity matrix. This can serve as a useful model for the trade and industry for prioritisation of export markets. New markets like Latin America, East European and Central Asian markets could be one of our obvious choices for an export thrust since there is a large measure of goodwill for India in these countries. SAPTA is another area for concentrated export effort.

The Ministry of Commerce has identified many countries as potential new markets for Indian products. Special incentives have been provided in the Export-Import Policy for promoting exports to these countries.

4.3.3 Other Measures

Ethical practices should be followed by Indian exporters. There have been instances when specific complaints have been brought to the Ministry's attention that some Indian exporters are not adhering to the rules and resorting to unethical business practices. An action should be taken against such business practices immediately.

Such actions not only reflect adversely on the entire Indian exporting community but ultimately on the nation as a whole. 'Made in India' label should be a symbol of quality, competitive price, reliability and service to the consumers.

4.4 Trade Policy Scenario

Trade policy of a country primarily aims at industrial and agricultural development, stability in domestic prices and augmentation and optimum utilisation of its foreign exchange resources. Such a trade policy is, however, influenced by international obligations of the country on account of its membership of international, regional and bilateral trade agreements and other multinational conventions and fora.

4.4.1 Regulation of Import and Export Trade

Trade policy involves regulation of import and export of the country. Such a regulation can be volumewise, valuewise, compositionwise and directionwise. It involves inter alia the following:

(i) Complete ban on import or export of some items;

(ii) Partial ban on import or export of some items.

(iii) Ensuring normal imports and exports trade undisturbed by internal or external factors.

4.4.1.1 Instruments of Trade Policy: The main instruments of trade policy are (i) tariffs; (ii) quantitative restrictions; (iii) para-tariff measures; (iv) subsidies and (v) miscellaneous administrative measures.

The tariff mechanism is used to ensure just and adequate protection to the domestic industry keeping in view the nascent stage of development of domestic industry. Anti-dumping measures help to provide safeguards to the domestic industry against unfair dumping of imports at below production cost which causes injury to domestic industry. These safeguard measures have been recently introduced.

The other instruments of Trade Policy also enable the levy of Quantitative Restrictions up to a ceiling limit on imports, provision of permitted subsidies to strengthen incentives for exports and administrative measures including state trading.

4.4.2 EXIM Policy

Till the beginning of the Second World War (1939-45), there was no control on India's imports and exports. Although there was no control on our foreign trade, there were certainly a number of regulations for keeping a watch on import and export transactions. The Government of India had imposed controls on some items of exports and also on some items of imports, intended primarily to meet the requirements of the second world war.

These control measures were supposed to be valid only till the end of the Second World War. However, even after the end of the war, the Government continued to control measures. During March 1947, an Act entitled 'Import and Export (Control) Act' was passed. This enactment had a life of forty-five years and three months.

In June, 1992, this act was superseded by the Foreign Trade (Development and Regulation) Act, 1992. The basic objective of the new Act was to give effect to the new liberalised export and import policy of the Government.

4.4.3 Five Year Import Export Policy

Till March 31, 1985, India's Import Policy used to be announced on yearly basis. Sometimes, this policy was even announced on 'six-monthly' basis. From April 1985 to March 1988, there was a three-year Import Policy. Subsequently, also three-year policies were announced, but each time the policy was cut short by one year. However, for the first time in the trade history of the country, a five year Export and Import Policy was announced by the Government of India on March 31, 1992. The announcement of the new EXIM Policy coincided with the launching of India's Eighth Five Year Plan. And on March 31, 1997, another EXIM Policy for the period 1997-2002 was announced. The current EXIM policy is co-terminus with our Ninth Five Year Plan.

4.4.4 Objectives of the EXIM Policy

The objectives of the current EXIM Policy are:

(a) Accelerating the country's transition to a globally oriented vibrant economy with a view to derive maximum benefits from expanding global market opportunities;

(b) Stimulating sustained economic growth by providing access to essential raw materials, intermediates, components, consumables and capital goods required for augmenting production;

(c) Enhancing the technological strength and efficiency of Indian agriculture, industry and services, thereby improving their competitive strength while generating new employment opportunities;

(d) Encouraging the attainment of internationally accepted standards of quality; and

(e) Providing consumers with good quality products and services at reasonable prices.

Emphasis in the current EXIM Policy is to enable the Indian industry to become technologically so strong that we can effectively meet global competition in the new millennium. The old stereotype objectives have been discarded.

4.5 New Trade Policy: Broad Outlook

The following are the highlights of new trade policy and how it will benefit the exporting community at large.

4.5.1 Agricultural Export Zones

With a view to providing rumenerative returns to the farming community in a sustained manner, efforts will be made to provide improved access to the produce/products of agriculture and allied sectors in the international market.

State governments may identify product specific agri export zone for end to end development for export of specific products from a geographically contiguous area. State government may evolve a comprehensive package of services provided by all State Government agencies, State agricultural universities and all institutions and agencies of the Union Government for intensive delivery in these zones.

Such services would include provision of pre/post harvest treatment and operations, plant protection, processing, packaging, storage and related research & development, etc. Department of Commerce will supplement, within its schemes and provisions, efforts of State Governments for facilitating such exports.

The service providers: setting up common infrastructural facilities such as sorting, grading, polishing, packaging, cold storage, transport equipment/refrigerated vans, vapour treatment heat treatment plant, X-ray screening facility etc. shall be entitled for EPCG Scheme.

Agri exporters shall be entitled for recognition as Export House/Trading House/Star Trading House/Super Star Trading house on achieving 1/3rd of the threshold limit prescribed for exporters of goods.

4.5.2 Market Access Initiative (MAI)

The government would assist the industry in research & development, market research, specific market and product studies, warehousing and retail marketing infrastructure in select country and direct market promotion activities through media advertising and buyer-seller meets. A plan scheme has been evolved for this purpose.

4.5.3 Special Economic Zones

- A new Chapter on Special Economic Zones introduced.
- Special Economic Zones developers are allowed duty free import/procurement from DTA for development of SEZ to give a boost for development of integrated infrastructure for exports.
- Duty free import/procurement from DTA of goods for setting up of factory in the Zone permitted.
- Items reserved for SSI do not require any licence for setting up units in SEZ.
- Units in SEZ can bring back their export proceeds in 365 days as against normal period of 180 days and can retain 100% of the proceeds in the EEFC account.
- Special Economic Zones trading units permitted to sell goods in the DTA in accordance with the import policy in force.
- Subcontracting of part of production abroad permitted.
- To facilitate greater flexibility and to attract capital intensive units into Special Economic Zones, amortisation of value of imported Capital Goods is being spread over a period of 8 years instead of 5 years at present.
- SEZ developer given infrastructure status under Income Tax Act as provided in the Finance Bill, 2001.

4.5.4 Removal of QRs

- The process of removal of import restrictions, which began in 1991, has been completed in a phased manner this year with removal of restrictions on 715 items. Out of these 715, 342 are textile products, 147 are agricultural products including alcoholic beverages and 226 are other manufactured products including automobiles.
- Import of agricultural products like wheat, rice, maize, other coarse cereals, copra and coconut oil has been placed in the category of State Trading. The nominated State Trading Enterprise will conduct the imports of these commodities solely as per commercial considerations. Similarly, import of petroleum products including petrol, diesel and ATF has also been placed in the category of State Trading. Import of urea will also be done through the mechanism of State Trading.
- Care has been taken to ensure a level playing field to domestic producers vis-à-vis imports. In conformity with the "National Treatment Principle" of GATT, imports have also been made subject to the following domestic regulations.

i) Import of all food products will be subject to compliance of all the provisions of Food Adulteration Act and Rules thereunder;

ii) Import of meat and poultry products will be subject to compliance of all the provisions of meat Food Product Order;

iii) Import Tea Waste will be subject to compliance of Tea Waste (Control Order);

iv) No import of textile material using the prohibited dyes like azo dye shall be allowed. For this purpose, a pre-shipment inspection certificate has been made mandatory.

- In view of road safety and environment considerations, imports of second hand automobiles have been allowed subject to the following conditions:

i) Import of automobiles older than three years is not allowed;

ii) Imported vehicles need to conform to Central Motor Vehicle Rules;

iii) Import of left hand drive vehicles not allowed;

iv) For ensuring the requirements, preshipment as well as post-shipment certification made mandatory;

v) Imported automobiles to have a minimum residual life of five years and the importer to ensure supply of spares and service during this period; and

vi) Such imports allowed only through customs port at Mumbai.

Similarly, import of new automobiles allowed subject to following conditions:

i) Import allowed only from the country of manufacture;

ii) Import of left hand drive vehicles not allowed;

iii) Imported vehicles to conform to the provisions of Motor Vehicles Act, 1988;

iv) Prototype of vehicle to be approved by notified agencies in India; and

- To ensure that import of agricultural products do not lead to unwanted infiltration of exotic diseases and pests in the country, it has been decided to subject import of primary products of plant and animal origin to "Bio Security & Sanitary and Phyto-Sanitary Permit' to be issued by Department. of Agriculture and Co-operation.

This permit will be based on Import Risk Analysis of the product to be conducted on scientific principles, in accordance with the WTO agreement on Application of Sanitary and Phyto-Sanitary Measures.

4.5.5 Export Promotion Capital Goods Scheme

- Imports of jigs, fixtures, dies, moulds to be allowed for the full CIF value of the licence instead of restricting to 20% of the CIF value of licence.
- Time limit of 180 days prescribed for finalisation of nexus by EPCG Committee failing which the nexus applied by the applicant becomes final.
- Extension in export obligation period under EPCG for licences issued during 1990-1996 upto 31.3.2002 upon execution of Bank Guarantee with the licensing authority.
- Extension in export obligation period for two years in respect of EPCG issued under Customs notification 29/1997 dated 1.4.1997 and 49/2000 dated 27.4.2000.
- No penalty for valuewise shortfall under EPCG except for the customs duty together with interest.
- Facility for partial fulfilment extended under EPCG scheme to reduce transaction time.
- For redemption, the licence holder has been extended the facility to submit either a consolidated statement signed by all banks or separate statements signed by individual banks.

4.5.6 Annual Advance Licence

- Extension of Annual Advance Licence facility for deemed exports and intermediate supplies.

- The entitlement for Annual Advance Licence increased from 125% to 200% of the FOB value of preceding year exports.
- Extension of Annual Advance Licence to other than Standard Input Output Norms exports.
- Clubbing facility for Annual Advance Licence.
- Dispensing with the need of technical characteristics for inputs except for items in the sensitive list.

4.5.7 Advance Licence

- Duty free import/procurement of fuel allowed under Standard Input Output Norms for sectors where the same cost more than 10% of the manufacturing cost.
- The facility of Advance Licences extended even to the cases where some of the inputs are supplied free of cost by the buyer.
- The entitlement for Advance licence where SION does not exist increased from 100% to 200% of the FOB value of preceding year exports for Export House/Trading House/Star Trading House/Super Star Trading House.
- Additional facility for Advance Licence where SION does not exist beyond entitlement as well against execution of Bank Guarantee.
- Dispensing with the need of technical characteristics for inputs except for items in the sensitive list.
- The facility of back to back LC for Advance Licence, which is presently confined to one bank and one branch, extended to cover any bank and branch.
- Revalidation of expired Advance Licences, where export obligation has been completed, by six months.

- 506 new Standard Input Output Norms fixed during 2000-01.
- No penalty for valuewise shortfall under Advance Licence except for the Customs duty together with interest provided the licence holder has achieved positive/minimum value addition.
- Coverage of additional ports under Advance Licence.
- Simplification of form relating to Advance Licence on SION.

4.5.8 Duty Free Replenishment Certificate Scheme

- Validity of DFRC to be extended from 12 months to 18 months.
- Dispensing with the need of technical characteristics for inputs except for items in the sensitive list.
- Automatic calculation of CIF value under DFRC scheme without reference to international price of individual inputs.
- Provision incorporated for claim of DFRC against advance payment.
- Coverage of additional ports under DFRC.
- Split up facility extended to DFRC scheme to give operational flexibility to the holder of DFRC.

4.5.9 Duty Entitlement Passbook Scheme

- Provision made for claiming DEPB against advance payment.
- Validity of DEPB extended upto the last day of the month in which the same is expiring.
- Rationalisation of DEPB rates in line with changes in Customs duty on account of union budget.
- Coverage of additional ports under DEPB.

- TRA facility extended to all notified ports under DEPB scheme.

4.5.10 EOU/EPZ/EHTP/STP Units

- NFPE/EP norms rationalised. EOU/EPZ units allowed to achieve minimum export Performance of 3 times the value of Central Government over 5 years instead of 5 times the value of Central Government, Highest NFEP requirement pegged at 10%.
- Supplies made to bonded warehouses set up under para 11.14 and 9.21 of the policy by EOU/EPZ units to be treated as exports for the purpose of domestic sales entitlement.
- Sub-contracting of production process abroad permitted. At present sub-contracting is permissible only within the country.
- DTA sale against foreign exchange, which is counted towards NFEP/EP is being confined to payment made from EEFC account of the buyer only.
- Simplification of procedure regarding utilisation of goods. EOU/EPZ units now have to account for duty free goods in over all terms and not consignment-wise. This is expected to facilitate ease in operation.
- E-Mail address is being made compulsory for approving EOU/EPZ units from 1.4.2001.
- Greater delegation to Development Commissioner's to approve EOU/EPZ projects. At present, Development Commissioners cannot approve project beyond US $20 million. This value restriction is being withdrawn.
- Suitable procedure provided for conversion of DTA units into EOU scheme having outstanding export obligation under advance licensing scheme by carrying

forward goods imported under advance Licensing Scheme.

- Joint Monitoring of EOU/EPZ units by a Committee consisting of DC and customs.

4.5.11 Gems and Jewellery Sector

- Extension of Diamond Dollar Account scheme (DDAS) to diamond studded jewellery exporters, having an average annual turnover of Rs 5 crore or above during the preceding three licensing years, allowing DDAS holders to operate up to five bank accounts (from maximum of two accounts prescribed earlier) and allowing non-DDAS to supply cut and polished diamonds to DDAS holder, which would counted towards discharge of his export obligations or entitle for a Replenishment licence as the case may be.
- With a view to facilitate certification/grading by international laboratories/agencies cut and polished diamonds weighing 0.50 carats and above, have been permitted for export and return of such diamonds for certification purposes.
- More flexibility to exporters under the Gold Loan Scheme by allowing exporters to fix the price and repay the gold loan within 180 days from the date of export subject to this price being also confirmed by the final buyer and the nominated agency supplying the gold.
- Exporters allowed to personally carry gems and jewellery of a value not exceeding US $ 2 million for purposes of holding/participating in overseas exhibitions.
- The foreign buyer scheme wherein precious metals can be supplied free of cost to the Indian manufacturers for

job working, has been extended to exporters having an annual average turnover of Rs. 5 crore during the preceding three years.

- The provisions of personal carriage of gems and jewellery export and import parcels is now available from Bangalore Airport also in addition to Delhi, Mumbai, Kolkata and Chennai.

4.5.12 Deemed Exports

- The suppliers have been given the option to file application either projectwise or covering supplies to all projects during a month/quarter or half yearly while claiming Terminal Excise duty/Drawback facility. They have also been given the option to file claim covering all the supplies to a project.
- A standard format prescribed for receipt of payment through normal banking channel.
- For supplies under paragraph 10.2(d)(e)(f) and (g) of the policy the sub-contractor has been given the facility to file Terminal Excise duty refund without waiting for payment from the main contractor.

Miscellaneous

- Double weightage for grant of status to the units exporting marine products with 'Q' mark Certification.
- Prospective/potential exporters allowed to become associate members of the export promotion councils.
- Free import of second hand capital goods upto 10 years old.

4.6 Transition to Market Friendly Economy

The process of liberalisation of Export-Import Policy is continuing. Our aim is to progressively remove barriers in the way of trade in a phased manner and put quantitative restrictions only on those export and import items which are required to be regulated either for security reasons or for environmental considerations. On a wider canvas, we are already moving towards integrating the Indian economy with the world economic order. The economic reforms policy initiated in India since 1991 is gathering momentum, reflecting India's intent to move towards a market economy. With rapid advances in communication and information technology, the globe is shrinking and India can ill-afford to be isolated or be cut off from the mainstream. De-regulation, de-centralisation and dismantling of tariff and non-tariff barriers is the order of the day. The sellers market fed on shortages has to make way for the buyers market. The Indian economy should, thus, find its rightful place in the comity of nations. In the new paradigm of globalisation, the emphasis is on competitive efficiency and consumer delight.

4.6.1 Promoting Software Exports

Though the Indian companies have been slowly moving up in the value chain, it has to be given more attention. They should concentrate more on developing products. The Indian companies should try to acquire domain knowledge and also try to move in vertical segments to take advantage of the expertise they have already acquired.

There should be a focused marketing approach i.e., marketing strategy. The lack of awareness of India's capabilities in international market is also hindering the exports. It has the advantage of low cost high quality services. The knowledge of this has to be spread in International markets. JETRO has recommended that the time is ripe for the Indian software industry to make a determined bid to enter the Japanese market, but this is also a period in which Indian exporters should take utmost care in quoting a price and adhering to the quality.

Indian companies should have a quality policy and should adhere to it. One measure in this direction was the recommendation by NASSCOM to make it mandatory for the software companies employing more than 10 professionals, to have ISO 9000 certification.

There is a lot of software in the public domain. The companies should acquire and adapt the software that is potentially applicable to their needs and which could minimise the re-development programmes already tested and in use elsewhere. Opportunities for modifying existing applications of software in order to develop relatively new commercially viable products appear greater in horizontal markets. There are many advantages in doing this as software packages for accounting, inventory control, administration project management, banking and information management already exist and can be modified.

The Indian companies should use effective and cost-efficient tools like Internet, direct marketing and should also tap niche markets. The role played by NASSCOM is a very important one. Though it is performing well, it can increase the marketing efforts by organising trade fairs/exhibitions etc.

Attention should also be given to the quality of the training the students are getting. There should be a central agency which would actively oversee the quality of education imparted.

Thus, it can be stated that with the software companies coming of age and with the government assistance that is provided, they should be able to exploit the opportunities existing in the international markets. The measures suggested above should also prove useful in boosting software exports and they should be able to achieve the set target of US $ 3.6 billion by the turn of the millennium.

4.6.2 Measures to Boost Exports of Agricultural Goods

India's agriculture is at a critical juncture. The sector occupies a strategic place in the country's overall economic development as it provides livelihood to almost two-thirds of the population. The most remarkable aspect of Indian agriculture is its diversified nature due to the climatic conditions. India has foodgrain crops, commercial crops, marine resources, aquaculture, floriculture, horticulture, animal husbandry etc.

Agricultural products which are presently being exported include tea, coffee, foodgrains (rice, coarse cereals and pulses), spices, tobacco, cashew, oilmeals, sesame and niger seeds, groundnut, sugar and molasses, fresh and processed fruits and juices, fish and fish products, meat and meat preparations and raw cotton.

During the 1950's, agricultural exports account for a half of the value of total exports of India. The share declined considerably in the second half of the 1960s. Not much variation was noticed in the 1970s except for two years viz. 1974-75 and 1975-76. In the new pattern of trade which emerged in the 1960's, the share of food and raw materials began to decline and that of manufactured items increased.

Although, India's exports of agricultural items have been on the increase, the full potential of agricultural exports has remained untapped and unexploited due to a variety of factors including the use of old farm technology on large areas of land that is cultivated, stagnation of output, rising domestic demand due to increasing population and income and lack of incentives at export promotion.

In addition, Indian agricultural sector suffers from many ailments. These include low growth rate, low productivity, low investment, low fertiliser consumption, inadequate credit availability and heavy dependence on monsoon.

Despite many short-comings including poor and outdated infrastructure and low investments, India's agricultural exports increased substantially from Rs. 13021 crore in 1993-94 to Rs. 24,239 crore in 1996-97 and improved marginally to Rs. 25419 crore in 1997-98. Agricultural exports constituted 20.4 per cent of total exports to world by India in 1996-97, and 18.8 per cent in 1997-98. Even the year 1998-99 witnessed a marginal increase in agricultural exports with exports rising to Rs. 26104 crore. However, the year 1999-2000 witnessed a downfall with exports dropping to Rs. 24576 crore, a decline of 9% over the previous year.

Despite inherent competitive strength of Indian agriculture, India's share in world exports of agricultural commodities is very low in many items (being less than 1 per cent) except the following items.

1. Tea and Mate 11.0 per cent
2. Spices 11.2 per cent
3. Rice 12.0 per cent
4. Animal foods 3.7 per cent
5. Fish and fish products 2.3 per cent
6. Pearls, precious and semi-precious stones 10.8 per cent
7. Iron ores and concentrates 7.8 per cent

8. Leather and its manufactures 3.5 per cent

It is further evident from these percentage shares that the potential for increasing agricultural exports from the country is very high provided it is backed up by various measures from the Government, industry and trade as also the foreign investors.

Studies carried out have clearly indicated that there is scope to accelerate exports and to achieve 25 to 30 per cent growth in terms of value or volume in respect of a number of items. Some of these include:

1. Aquaculture
2. Floriculture
3. Fresh fruits
4. Tomato Paste and Products
5. Tropical fruit juices
6. Pulp and concentrates
7. Preserved mushrooms
8. Rice
9. Spices
10. Sugar
11. Molasses
12. Alcohol including Ethyl
13. Meat
14. Poultry, and
15. Milk

In order to realise the full export potential of agricultural sector, it is necessary to facilitate flow of investments to strengthen the infrastructure. Agricultural sector needs to be given export orientation.

India has one of the longest coast lines in the world and Indian ports need to be developed comparable with ports of Singapore and Hongkong to handle the goods efficiently and effectively and to offer handling charges at very comparative rates. Indian ports have to handle large tonnage than what is being done currently. The daily loading capacity at the Indian Ports hovers around 3000 to 4000 tonnes which is 11 per cent of what ports of developed Asian countries handle.

Lack of proper loading facilities, scarcity of modern warehousing capacity near ports, shortage of railway wagons for ferrying goods are adversely affecting competitiveness of India's exports. For example, rice and de-oiled cake exporters complain that they do not get railway wagons to carry their goods to the ports. In the case of fruits and vegetables, lack of storage capacity is obviously affecting the utilisation of fruits and vegetables and their exports. The Cold Storage Act is known to be working as a deterrent to the holding of stocks. Estimates are that more than Rs. 5000 crore worth of fruits and vegetables get wasted each year due to lack of storage and transportation facilities.

The strategy for increasing exports of agricultural goods includes:

- Jettison the present policy which prescribes that only those farm products should be exported in which the country has a surplus.

- Removal of physical barriers (particularly in cereals) on quantities to be exported.

- Trade Policy for the farm sector should be open, free and outward looking with complete freedom to the farmer to dispose off his produce without any Government restrictions on quantity, prices, etc. (cotton exports from the country are controlled by quotas monitored by the Textile Commissioner).

- Investment, public, private and foreign into infrastructure, need to be encouraged to boost agro-exports

(exports of fruits and vegetables could be increased manifold if refrigeration facilities are created at all points of storage at the farm level, during transportation and also at airports). Investments in agriculture have to be stepped up substantially, as a percentage of the total expenditure, five year plans, on a continuous basis.

- Abolish all export controls and regulations like canalisation.

- Persistent efforts are required in the areas of post-harvest technology in order to preserve and utilise the produce both for domestic consumption and export purposes (wastage of fruits and vegetables, if prevented, would lead to greater availability for production and exports). To promote farm production and to encourage agro-based industries, the farm sector should be given the status of an industry with all the facilities including cheap credit, specialised funding institutions, storage and marketing facilities.

- Agriculture sector should be excluded from taxes including capital gains tax.

- Foreign capital and technology should be encouraged liberally.

- Eastern states need to be geared to increase production of various agricultural commodities with the help of improved techniques.

- Productivity of various crops needs to be increased as land resources are likely to be scarcer in future. India has lower agricultural productivity at around 1.6 tonnes average yield per hectare, which is lower to that of not only developed countries but also to that of developing countries like China, Indonesia, Bangladesh, Mexico and Brazil. To achieve a high agricultural growth rate the average yield has to be 2.5 tonnes or more per hectare.

- Agricultural growth has to be substantially stepped up to over 3.5 per cent to 6 per cent in output terms. Efforts should be made to achieve doubling of farm production within the next 15 years which require an average annual growth rate of 4.7 per cent.

- Irrigation system need to be improved, strengthened and expanded so as to reduce drastically the dependence of agriculture on monsoon. Minor irrigation needs to be promoted very widely.

- State Governments should amend the Agricultural Land Ceilings Acts.

- Fertiliser consumption has to be promoted to increase production to meet the increasing domestic requirements and exports. Profitability of farming operations could be increased only through higher productivity. Use of bio-fertilisers, bio-pesticides, organic manures and micro-nutrients has to be promoted vigorously.

- Government should not lose any time in getting the approval of the Plant Varieties Protection Bill as that would safeguard the interests of farmers. India should not avail of the five-year transitional period provided in the World Trade Agreement and go straight away for plant protection regime. Production of high-value seeds involves the process of hand pollination which is highly labour intensive and India would stand to gain.

- In order to protect and promote farmer's interest commodity exchanges need to be set up.

To conclude, it can be said that the inclusion of agriculture in the Uruguay Round Trade Negotiations which finally led to the conclusion of an Agreement on Agriculture and the setting up of the World Trade Organisation have opened up new vistas for trade but it has also created new problems, some of which are quite formidable for the developing countries. Agricultural exports have been severely constrained due to tariff barriers, export subsidies and quotas. Products from many developing countries including India suffer from non-competitiveness on account of export subsidies in other countries.

In the Post-WTO era, developed countries are coming up with many non-tariff trade barriers. Plant, animal and human health have become important areas of concern for the developed countries leading to new health regulations and food safety standards. India has to cope up with sanitary and phyto-sanitary provisions of the agreement on agriculture and also the patenting norms and issues relating to intellectual property rights and plant variety protection.

While efforts to strengthen Indian agricultural sector to make it globally competitive should continue, it becomes necessary for India to fulfil the obligations and commitments as per the Uruguay Round Agreement on Agriculture. The existing provisions of the global agreement on agricultural trade came up for fresh scrutiny in the next round of international negotiations which started in Seattle, USA, in December 1999. The WTO Conference at Seattle failed because agriculture was the main stumbling block. Unless the developed world cuts down appreciably its export subsidy, developing countries have little hope of gaining from global agricultural trade.

India should consider removal of some important agricultural items out of the negative list in the shortest period possible. All industrialised nations are seeking better terms for removal of agricultural products out of the restricted list of imports. They have been asking India to take prompt steps in bringing down high tariff in many agricultural products to help better market opportunities to other WTO members.

In the larger interests of India's foreign trade and commitments made under the Uruguay Round Agreement, it will be necessary for India to remove quantitative restrictions on imports. As of now, India's offer to remove the quantitative restrictions on import in six years period has been rejected by the WTO's Balance of payments (BOP) Committee. The potential of exports of agricultural commodities from the country on a modest scale is estimated at Rs. 50,000 crore by the turn of the century. Realisation of this potential, however, will be possible if sizeable investments from the public and private sectors and foreign investors go into agriculture particularly to strengthen the infrastructure on one hand and to enhance production on the other.

4.7 Conclusions

India is determined to raise its share in world trade to 1 per cent. The total world export is expected to be around US$ 7.5 trillion in 2004. For India to achieve 1 per cent share it requires a total export figure of US$ 75 billion from the current levels of US$ 43 billion. The task is hard but not unachievable, for which appropriate steps and measures must be taken and the Government is preparing itself in this direction.

As is evident from the above analysis, the measures include improving infrastructural facilities, exploring new markets and making relevant and necessary changes in the Export Import Policy. Apart from these steps, measures are also being taken to boost the exports.

Although India's agricultural exports witnessed a negative growth in the year 1999-2000, yet agricultural products have very good scope for improvement and also have a large share in the world exports. It is also very important to realise that globalisation has brought tremendous competition which in turn brings in better products and services to customers. In order to survive and grow in a competitive world, the secret lies in how fast one can get to the market place with the new products. This is going to be the new wave of the future particularly when we enter into the new millennium [2].

One way of getting started to face the new challenges is by realising the importance of Four P's of the Quality Management Plan - i.e. 1. the People, 2. the Product, 3. the Processes and 4. the Profits.

If India wants to be a global player, it has to reach global standards by adopting globally acceptable standards. Through quality alone, the product excellence will come ultimately. In order to face global competition which at times is very fierce and cut throat developing and adopting a right type of attitude i.e., a different mindset through quality culture is the only way out. India's quality dream can be fulfilled only when 'Made in India' label proves a symbol of quality in other countries. This can be achieved only when the emphasis is shifted from management of quality to quality management.

Notes

1. Indian Institute of Foreign Trade, *Global Economic Challenges in the New Millennium: India's Strategic Agenda*, 1998.

2. Joseph and Susan Berk, *Total Quality Management* (Excel Books, 1993).

Chapter 5

WTO and Developing Countries: Impact on India's Foreign Trade

5.1 General Background

It was originally intended that the post-war international economic order would consist of three institutions; the World Bank, the International Monetary Fund (IMF) and an International Trade Organisation (ITO). Although the first two were successfully established in 1944, the ITO never came into being. Due to opposition within the United States, the founding document of the ITO, the Charter of Havana (1947), was never ratified. However, the need for an international body to administer global trading rules was still widely recognised. The General Agreement on Tariffs and Trade (GATT) was signed in 1947 at Geneva by 23 countries including India. The provisions contained in the Charter of Havana, came into force on 1 January 1948.

At the time of its inception, the main objective of GATT was establishment of a world trading regime in which countries would gradually liberalise trade among themselves. Therefore, reduction of tariffs on trade in manufactures was adopted as a major goal for GATT.

Since then, eight rounds of multilateral trade negotiations have been held in order to further liberalise world trade. At the conclusion of the 8th (Uruguay) Round, there were 123 GATT contracting parties, and this had increased to 128 by early 1995.

Over the years, GATT evolved as the only instrument that laid down a set of multilaterally agreed rules to govern international trade. It also functioned as a multilateral forum for discussions and negotiations on trade policy issues through which attempts were made in making the trading environment more predictable and liberalised.

With the aim of achieving the progressive liberalisation of world trade, the GATT adopted a number of basic principles, that of non-discrimination being the most fundamental. This principle is implemented in the form of the most favoured nation clause (MFN). The MFN (Most Favoured Nation) clause is the essence of GATT through which contracting parties grant each other equality of treatment in order to ward off uncontrolled and arbitrary protectionism. Other principles are: more favourable treatment for developing countries, elimination of qualitative restrictions and prohibition of export subsidies, tariffs as the only legal instrument of protection, transparency in national trade legislation.

The functioning and achievements of GATT, had however, been subjects of a polemical debate. Often referred as the 'rich nations' club', GATT had been accused of ignoring the problems of developing countries.

5.2 The Uruguay Round

The Uruguay Round, launched in Punta del Este in September 1986, was the most challenging ambitious and protracted in the history of GATT. The Uruguay Round - the eighth round of trade negotiations - proved to be the most ambitious and complex trade negotiations under GATT because of the paradigm shift in its agenda. The negotiations covered three aspects of international trade:

- Firstly, they aimed to improve market access by unprecedented and far-reaching tariff cuts. Measures were also taken to reduce non-tariff barriers, in particular technical regulations motivated by domestic political considerations. All aspects of agricultural policy were brought into GATT.

- Secondly, GATT's field of application was extended to include new sectors, not previously dealt within multilateral trade negotiations, such as: the agreements on Trade - Related Aspects of Intellectual Property Rights (TRIPS), on Trade in Services (GATS), on Public Procurement Markets and on Trade-related Investment Measures (TRIMS).

- Thirdly, GATT trade protection measures were revised, particularly antidumping and anti-subsidy measures, measures based on the Article XIX safeguard clause, customs valuation, rules of origin and export licenses.

The new issues of services, investment and intellectual property rights were included in the Uruguay Round for negotiations. Further, there were two sectors in the area of goods - that is, textiles and agriculture - which had received less attention in the past but were taken up for negotiations in the eighth round. Despite a diversity of negotiating issues, the Uruguay Round proposed an integrated dispute settlement mechanism for various areas. An incisive analysis of the initiatives taken for launching the Uruguay Round, no doubt, evinces that the interests of developing countries were not taken into consideration - only compliance to desired objectives were expected from the developing countries.

The developed countries set the tune for imposing industrial commercial and financial liberalisation on developing countries by arguing that the latter's state interventions and social policies are barriers to trade. The emphasis in the Uruguay Round, therefore, has been relatively less on reduction of barriers to trade in goods than on the enlargement of the coverage of issues and areas under GATT.

5.3 Effect on India

The dilemma of the developing countries had been the predicament of India during the Uruguay Round negotiations. The main issues of concern for India revolved around Agriculture, Trade Related Intellectual Property Rights (TRIPs), the Multi-Fibre Arrangement (MFA) in textiles, Trade Related Investment Measures (TRIMs), the General Agreement on Trade in Services (GATS), and the Integrated Dispute Settlement Mechanism under GATT.

It has been argued that the Agreement severely militates against several Indian laws. The apprehension is that GATT would have an adverse effect on India's sovereignty and development priorities.

5.4 The Creation of the WTO

The World Trade Organisation (WTO) started its activities on 1 January 1995.

5.4.1 General

As the global economy becomes even more integrated, the proper implementation of rules governing the multilateral trading system has become increasingly important. In response to the perceived inability of the GATT to act as an effective guarantor of such rules, the states participating in the Uruguay Round agreed to create a new and stronger international organisation to oversee world trade. The WTO framework, an international organisation in its own right, substantially differs from the GATT's provisional Treaty in the sense that it administers a unified package of agreements to which all members are committed; it brings new areas of co-operation into the multilateral trading system and it introduces a new dispute settlement procedure.

The WTO agreements are negotiated and signed by the bulk of the world's trading nations and ratified in their parliaments. Compared to GATT, the WTO is much more powerful because of its institutional foundation and its dispute settlement system. Countries that do not abide by its trade rules are taken to court and can eventually face retaliation.

Until the Uruguay Round, which ended in 1994, the trade negotiations focused on non-agricultural goods, mainly because the U.S. wanted to protect its farm sector. Over the years, as the corporate interests of the developed countries have expanded, these countries have also lobbied for more issues to be incorporated into GATT/WTO. Its agenda now includes agriculture, services (financial, telecommunications, information technology, etc.), intellectual property rights, electronic commerce and possibly in the next round, investment, government procurement and competition policy.

Changes in rules come about mainly through multilateral negotiations called 'rounds'. Each round offers a package approach to trade negotiations, in which many issues are negotiated together and trade-offs between different issues are made. Between the rounds, negotiations on single issues take place.

The Dispute Settlement Mechanism (DSM) is probably the most important element of the WTO. It seeks to provide security and predictability with formal legal proceedings.

The details of the DSM are set out in the understanding on Rules and Procedures, Governing the Settlement of Disputes. The main accomplishments of the DSM refer to the settlement of disputes with greater transparency, in a fair and impartial manner. For example, the DSM is now the sole authority to establish panels. Also there now has to be a consensus against the establishment of panels or the adoption of panel reports for these decisions not to be made. A further innovation is the possibility of appealing against a final report to a permanent Appellate Body. Finally, the WTO may sanction cross-retaliation as a last resort.

Today, the WTO has 140 members (as on April 2001) . Out of these 140 member nations, 27 are categorised as the least developed countries (LDCs). One of the commonly used yardsticks to measure the success of the WTO is the volume of world trade. The results seem to be excellent as the world trade has gone up by 25% in the last 4 years. But the benefits of increased trade are not widely shared. For example, the LDCs represent 20% of the world's population, but they generate a mere 0.03% of the trade flows.

5.4.2 Competence

The WTO will seek to achieve its objectives in carrying out the following tasks: oversee and facilitate the implementation of all agreements and legal instruments negotiated in connection with the Uruguay Round; provide a forum for all negotiations among members concerning their multilateral trade relations; administer the Trade Policy Review Mechanism (TPRM) reviewing trade policies of WTO members every two years; cooperate with the IMF and the International Bank for Reconstruction and Development

(IBRD) to achieve greater coherence in global economic policy making.

5.4.3 Structure

The WTO is headed by a Ministerial Conference, formed of representatives of all the members, which has overall responsibility for the organisation and has the authority to take decisions on all matters under any of the Multilateral Trade Agreements. The General Council, also formed of representatives of all members, carries out the functions of the WTO between meetings of the Ministerial Conference. The General Council is also given the task of establishing and overseeing three specialised councils for Trade in Goods, Trade in Services and Trade-Related Aspects of Intellectual Property Rights.

The Agreement also provides for the following committees. Trade and Development, Trade and Environment, Balance of Payments Restrictions and Budget, Finance and Administration. The Administration of the WTO will be the responsibility of the WTO Secretariat, which is headed by a Director General.

Numerous specialised committees, working groups and working parties deal with individual agreements and other areas such as the environment development, membership applications and regional trade agreements.

The first Ministerial Conference in Singapore in 1996 added three new working groups to this structure. They deal with the relationship between trade and investment, the interaction between trade and competition policy and transparency in government procurement.

At the second Ministerial Conference in Geneva in 1998, members decided that the WTO would also study the area of electronic commerce or more popularly known as e-commerce, a task to be shared out among existing councils and committees.

5.4.4 Objectives

The objectives of the WTO as laid down in the Preamble to the Marrakesh Agreement are much the same as those of the GATT, i.e. raising standards of living and incomes; ensuring full employment; expanding production and trade; and making optimal use of the world's resources. Three significant additions are made: all the objectives now apply also to trade in services as well as to trade in goods, the concept of 'sustainable development' is included in the commitment to help make optimal use of the world's resources; there is a formal recognition of the need to assist developing countries in securing a greater share in the growth of international trade.

The WTO is the only global international organisation dealing with the rules of trade between nations. The goal is to help producers of goods and services, exporters, and importers conduct their business. Its main function is to ensure that trade flows as smoothly, predictably and freely as possible. The result is assurance. Consumers and producers know that they can enjoy secure supplies and greater choice of the finished products, components, raw materials and services that they use. Producers and exporters know that foreign markets will remain open to them.

Summing up, WTO's overriding objective is to help trade flow smoothly, freely, fairly and predictably. It does this by,

- Administering trade agreements
- Acting as a forum for trade negotiations
- Settling trade disputes

- Reviewing national trade policies

-Assisting developing countries in trade policy issues, through technical assistance and training programmes.

- Co-operating with other international organisations.

5.5 WTO Agreements

The WTO's rules - the agreements - are the result of negotiations between the members. The current set were the outcome of the 1986-94 Uruguay Round negotiations which included a major revision of the original General Agreement on Tariffs and Trade (GATT).

GATT is now the WTO's principal rule-book trade in goods. The Uruguay Round also created new rules for dealing with trade in services, relevant aspects of intellectual property, dispute settlement, and trade policy reviews. Through these agreements, WTO members operate a non-discriminatory trading system that spells out their rights and their obligations. Each country receives guarantees that its exports will be treated fairly and consistently in other countries' markets. Each promises to do the same for imports into its own market. The system also gives developing countries some flexibility in implementing their commitments.

Goods: It all began with trade in goods. From 1947 to 1994, GATT was the forum for negotiating lower customs duty rates and other trade barriers. The text of General Agreement spells out important rules, particularly non-discrimination.

Since 1995, the updated GATT has become the WTO's umbrella agreement for trade in goods. It has annexes dealing with specific sectors such as agriculture and textiles, and with specific issues such as state trading, product standards, subsidies and actions taken against dumping.

Services: Banks, insurance firms, telecommunications companies, tour operators, hotel chains and transport companies looking to do business abroad can now enjoy the same principles of freer and fairer trade that originally only applied to trade in goods. These principles appear in the new General Agreement on Trade in Services (GATS). WTO members have also made individual commitments under GATS stating which of their services sectors they are willing to open to foreign competition, and how open those markets are.

Intellectual Property: The WTO's intellectual property agreement amounts to rules for trade and investment in ideas and creativity. The rules state how copyrights, trademarks, geographical names used to identify products, industrial designs, integrated circuit layout-designs and undisclosed information such as trade secrets - "intellectual property" - should be protected when trade is involved.

Dispute Settlement: The WTO's procedure for resolving trade quarrels under the Dispute Settlement Understanding is vital for enforcing the rules and therefore for ensuring that trade flows smoothly. Countries bring disputes to the WTO if they think their rights under the agreements are being infringed. Judgements by specially-appointed independent experts are based on interpretations of the agreements and individual countries' commitments. The system encourages countries to settle their differences through consultation.

Policy Review: The Trade Policy Review Mechanism's purpose is to improve transparency, to create a greater understanding of the policies that countries are adopting, and to assess their impact. Many members also see the reviews as constructive feedback on their policies. All WTO members must undergo periodic scrutiny, each review containing reports by the country concerned and the WTO Secretariat. Over 45 members have been reviewed since the WTO came into force.

5.6 WTO and the Developing Countries

Over three-quarters of WTO members are developing or least developed countries. Special provisions for these members are included in all the WTO agreements. The special provisions include:

- longer time periods for implementing agreements and commitments,
- measures to increase trading opportunities for these countries,
- provisions requiring all WTO members to safeguard the trade interests of century countries,
- and support to help developing countries build the infrastructure for WTO work, handle disputes, and implement technical standards.

A committee on trade and development, assisted by a sub-committee on least-developed countries, looks at developing countries' special needs. Its responsibility includes implementing of the agreements, technical co-operation, and the increased participation of developing countries in the global trading system.

5.6.1 WTO and Developing Countries - Face to Face

The following are the reasons for the developing countries having little power within the WTO framework:

1. Although developing countries make up three-fourths of WTO membership and by their vote can in theory influence the agenda and outcome of trade negotiations, they have never used this to their advantage. Most developing country economies are in one way or another dependent on the U.S., the E.U., or Japan in terms of imports, exports, and security etc. Any obstruction of a consensus at the WTO might threaten the overall well-being and security of dissenting developing nations.

2. Trade negotiations are based on the principle of reciprocity or 'trade-offs'. That is, one country gives a concession in an area, such as the lowering of tariffs for a certain product, in return for another country acceding to a certain agreement. This type of bartering benefits the large and diversified economies because they can get more by giving more. For the most part, negotiations and trade-offs take place among the developed countries and some of the richer or larger developing countries.

3. Developing countries have fewer human and technical resources. Many cannot cope with the 40-50 meetings held in Geneva each week. Hence they often enter negotiations less prepared than their developed country counterparts.

4. Developing countries have discovered that seeking recourse in the dispute settlement system is costly and requires a level of legal expertise that they may not have. Furthermore, the basis on which the system is run - whether a country is violating free trade rules - is not the most appropriate for their development needs.

5. The agenda of the WTO, the implementation of its agreements, and the much-praised dispute settlement system all serve to advance the interests of developed countries, sidelining those of the developing countries.

6. The LDCs are marginalised in the world trade system, and their products continue to face tariff escalation.

7. Rules uniformly applied to WTO members have brought about inequalities because each member has different economic circumstances.

5.6.2 Achievements Under WTO

The first ministerial conference of the WTO was held in Singapore in December 1996. The conference adopted a declaration concerning the implementation of the Uruguay Round agreements the agenda for the WTO's future work, the relationship between trade and the environment and between trade and competition, investment-related issues and internationally recognised labour standards.

The conclusion of the WTO agreement on basic telecommunications in 1997 was another major achievement. This agreement involves 69 countries from every continent accounting for more than 93% of world revenues from telecommunication services. The WTO negotiations on financial services were successfully completed by the end of 1997. All major trading partners, including the USA, are parties to the agreement and many have submitted significantly improved commitments for both market access and national treatment for companies operating in the territory of another WTO member.

5.6.3 The Seattle Failure

The WTO meeting held at Seattle was a failure and a profound disappointment for the EC, in particular. The reasons for its failure could be summarised below:

(a) The ground had been inadequately prepared in the run up to Seattle. As a result, divergences continued up to and through Seattle.

(b) Added to the above was the lack of time available for serious negotiations, difficulties in the management and organisation of the Conference, disruption on the streets and the exclusion of many developing countries from the discussions.

5.6.4 Initiative for Institutional Reforms Under WTO

After the Seattle round it was widely felt that WTO needs to work in a more inclusive and transparent way vis-à-vis all members and improve communication to the outside world. There should be greater participation by developing countries. Perhaps the future meetings of WTO should include following basic components:

5.6.4.1 Market Access: Everyone benefits from greater market access for their products and services, in order to increase economic growth. It was clear at Seattle that only a comprehensive approach to market access, covering all sectors, can enable all Members to exploit their comparative advantage and thus increase their trade. India, for example, needs better access for services providers and reduction in textile tariff peaks - to take two obvious examples. This is only achievable in a broad round context.

5.6.4.2 Rules: The WTO also needs to update its rules to respond to the effects of globalisation, so our traders and investors can enjoy a predictable, transparent and non-discriminatory framework. Basic rules on investment and competition are necessarily part of such an agenda. It was not possible to begin negotiations on these two subjects of such systemic importance. It is also a pity that it was not possible to begin negotiations on trade facilitation, on improvements to rules in trade defence or technical barriers to trade, all of which would contribute to more predictable market access conditions.

5.6.4.3 Development: Seattle highlighted the need to better integrate developing countries into the trading system through better market access, improved special and differential treatment, better co-ordinated capacity building, and a more active role within the WTO mechanisms. A new round would enable the developing countries' trade agenda - including more sensitive issues - to be comprehensively addressed. As in Seattle, the EU remains willing to take on board a comprehensive development agenda for the WTO. The question is, however, whether it is in developing countries' long term interest to pursue a development agenda relying on opt outs from WTO disciplines - to many, it seems the antithesis of integration.

5.6.4.4 Civil Society: The WTO must still answer questions of public concern. Societies remain concerned over the potential influence of the trading system on the social and environmental dimension of economic development, and on public health and consumer protection, and seek answers that both safeguard the trading system and these societal concerns. Many developing countries including India are concerned about social justice, the development dimension of trade, the impact of globalisation. WTO motives are to bring greater predictability and clarity into international trade rules. There is a need to work harder to demonstrate that WTO agenda will not lead to protectionist outcomes.

5.7 Impact of GATT and WTO on India's Foreign Trade

Currently, India's share in world export is 0.6 per cent, and in world imports also it is 0.6 per cent. Under the *cetris paribus* assumption, considering the market share, India's exports is to increase by US $ 1.5 billion to US $ 2 billion per year in the first two to three years of implementation of GATT accord, which may basically emerge from the liberalisation of MFN tariffs in agriculture and textiles, etc. The annual gain that may accrue to India from trade liberalisation in the Uruguay Round could work out US $ 4.6 billion by 2002.

The global trade on the whole may grow by about 9-10 per cent from 1995 onwards till the end of this decade. In other words, it is expected to grow to $ 7 trillion from the current value of $ 3.8 trillion. The additional gains may go up to $ 450 billion per annum towards the end of the decade.

The three main sectors which will witness developments because of the WTO agreement implementation are agriculture, textiles and the pharmaceutical sector. A brief analysis of the likely impact on these sectors is discussed below.

5.7.1 The Agricultural Sector

Tariffs in the agricultural sector will be reduced substantially (i.e. by about one third of the current rate). The reduction of agricultural subsidies in the rich countries by as much as 20 per cent to 36 per cent over a six year period, should increase the market for our agricultural products globally. Thus, India would have a competitive edge by virtue of its low price and quality.

It is projected that exports of Indian agricultural products will benefit by additional $ 850 million in the first three years and it may go up to $ 1.2 billion towards the end of the decade.

The GATT accord stipulates reduction or withdrawal of two types of subsidies" 'Non-Product Specific' subsidies, and 'Product-Specific' subsidies. Non-product specific subsidies cover inputs like fertilisers, water, seeds, pesticides, and agricultural credit etc. According to the final agreement, these subsidies have to be limited to 10 per cent of the value of total agricultural production.

Due to subsidy reduction commitments as agreed upon in the Uruguay Round, India will be able to export more in the enlarged global market. This is due to decline in prices for reduction in tariffs and agricultural subsidies.

The products likely to benefit include rice, wheat and wheat preparation, tobacco, fruits and vegetables, juice and juice concentration, milk and milk products, tropical products etc.

Indian Public Distribution System (PDS) will, however, remain unaffected from the subsidy reduction commitments.

However, India's potential to export would depend upon the dynamism of governmental policy towards agricultural exports as well as on the ability to meet the strict sanitary and phytosanitary standards meant for such exports. To exploit the tremendous potential in horticulture and floriculture, considerable efforts are required in the areas of infrastructure, institutional and legal framework. Government must consider increasing the ceiling on land holdings for the purposes of increasing agricultural exports.

5.7.2 The Textile Industry

Trade in textiles and clothing is presently governed by an agreement known the Multi-Fibre agreement (MFA), under which countries such as USA, EU maintain quantitative restrictions on the import of textile items from developing countries like India. This agreement worked against India because India has a vibrant textile industry which produces goods matching world standards. This means that bilateral negotiations pertaining to quota allocation will also get eliminated and the entire textile trade would come under the free trade regime, governed by the rules applicable to trade in other goods.

The integration of the textile trade into GATT system, has provided India with,

(a) a higher growth target for textile exports than was possible under the Multi-Fibre Agreement (MFA);

(b) the inclusion of additional items under the quota system which would mean an expanded market for another 10 years, quite favourable for India.

However, the future of the textile industry would depend on the emerging competitive advantage in the global market accruing to India's competitors in the South East Asian region. Although non-quota markets suffer from their small size and low buying power, India will have to tap non-quota markets for cotton textiles. The forty years of protectionist policies have rendered India's textile industry uncompetitive in world market. In order to benefit from the liberalised trade regime, the Government will have to reorient the complete textile policy.

Under the GATT agreement, India is committed to reducing the average tariff levels on 17 textile products from the current 85 per cent to about 40 per cent over a 10 year period. The items on which India has agreed to lower tariff fall into three categories, namely,

(a) fabrics made from flex;

(b) special woven fabrics; and,
(c) felt and non-woven materials.

After the phasing out of the MFA, it is expected that world exports of textiles will go up by $ 25 billion per year. At present, international trade in textiles is $ 240 billion a year.

At present, India's textile exports constitute 2.5 per cent of world trade in textiles. The share is expected to rise to 7.2 per cent by the year 2000. Additional gains will be $ 400 million in the first phase of dismantling of the MFA. By the end of the decade (second phase of dismantling of MFA), the gains are expected to grow to $ 700 million.

As a result of new GATT Accord on textiles, Indian exports of cotton garments will increase substantially in quantity as well as value terms. According to new accord, India's potential gain in textile trade will be the maximum. Average textile import of developed countries is around US $ 66 billion of which US $ 33 billion from developing countries. Since one-third of India's total exports consist of textiles only, it is expected that the accord will certainly increase its market share from the current level of 2.4 per cent to 4 per cent.

The realities of multilateralism require countries like India to change administrative and institutional arrangements for effective governance. Problems would arise if national legislations are not aligned to GATT provisions. Therefore, the operational difficulties in governance by developing countries like India for tackling systematic differences in national priorities and international requirements would be enormous. For instance, India will have to replace trade distorting policies with trade-oriented measures, and transparency in administration of policies would be required. However, it must be mentioned that such changes have not only been demanded by overseas investors but also by Indian entrepreneurs.

5.7.3 TRIPS

The main proposal which the GATT encourages, is a universal product patent. GATT recognises that any new product would have to be patented, and royalties have to be paid to the country or company or individual who invented the product.

Two important features of TRIP negotiations are (i) Change from the patenting of process to patenting of products regarding drugs, foods and chemicals, and (ii) patenting of seeds.

As a result of change from process patent to product patent it is feared that drug prices will rise rapidly. It should be noted that less than 10 per cent of the list of essential drugs is currently protected through patents, i.e. most commonly used drugs are off-patent. Therefore, increase in price can occur only in the case of new drugs.

The Indian drug and pharmaceutical industry has grown and flourished under the protection of process patents instead of the internationally accepted product patents. Therefore, Indian patent laws have to be drastically overhauled at the earliest to align them with globally pervasive laws. In view of the proposed patent regime, Indian drug industry will have to invest considerably in research and development (R & D).

Again, much would depend on the Government's drug policy. Control on drug industry's overall profitability will have to be liberalised to enable Indian companies to plough back profits into R & D activities. Therefore, Drug Price

Control Order (DPCO) will have to be made more flexible in its functioning.

5.7.4 The Services Sector

India's exports of services were $ 5.5 billion in 1992. Its share in world's export of services is 0.5 per cent and at present it is growing by 16 per cent per annum. It is estimated to grow by about 25 per cent from 1995. The gains from GATT accord would be about $ 400 million in the first 3 years and it will reach $ 1.4 billion towards the end of the decade. The services which will gain include computer software, engineering services, medical and para-medical, processing of insurance claims, legal services, films, legal and financial consultancy and banking.

5.8 Improving the Functioning of WTO

Seven years after the conclusion of the Uruguay Round, it appears appropriate to consider possible improvements in the functioning of the WTO system. There is a view that, in overall terms, the WTO is performing its mandate in a generally satisfactory manner. There are, however, valid reasons to seriously consider institutional improvements. The challenges raised by the process of globalisation make it imperative for all institutions to adapt their functioning to the growing complexity of the issues falling under their mandate.

At the same time, as the WTO comes closer to becoming a universal organisation, there is a need to further consider how to ensure both effectiveness and transparency in a manner which fosters participation by all WTO members. Moreover, all these changes are taking place in political context in which trade policy issues are increasingly a matter of public interest.

Following the Seattle Ministerial, particular attention has been given to the issue of how to ensure internal transparency and effective participation of all Members. The Chairman of the General Council has been conducting informal consultations on these issues and a large number of delegations have presented written and oral contributions. Discussions have shown that delegations share the view that there is no need to envisage changes that would alter the basic character of the organisation and its decision-making process. In particular, decisions should continue to be made by consensus, in accordance with article IX of the WTO agreement. At the same time, there is a clear interest in seeking a number of improvements in WTO functioning, in order to achieve enhanced effectiveness, transparency and participation. Broadly speaking, many of the suggestions made can be classified under three headings:

(a) Measures to improve decision-making, including issues relating to the organisation and functions of informal consultations;

(b) Measures to foster the flow of information and participation by all members;

(c) Measures to improve Ministerial meetings and the General Council.

At the same time, it is worth recalling paragraph 4 of the 1998 Ministerial Declaration which said: "We recognise the importance of enhancing public understanding of the benefits of the multilateral trading system in order to build support for it and agree to work towards this end. In this context, we will consider how to improve the transparency of WTO operations". So far, however, no action has been taken in the General Council to implement this mandate. The EC presented a communication on the issue of external transparency in July 1998 and has presented additional ideas in informal submissions to the General Council. It is considered that further progress on external transparency would reinforce the role of WTO as an institution without, in any way, affecting its inter-governmental nature.

We now discuss, hereby, on how to improve the functioning of the WTO both as regards internal transparency and effective participation and on external transparency. Perhaps there are important synergies between both aspects of WTO functioning and both of them require appropriate consideration in the General Council. Indeed, it is essential that issues relating to the institutional functioning of the WTO be discussed as "systemic questions" which require open consideration by WTO members, outside any possible negotiating context.

1. Measures to improve decision-making including issues relating to the organisation and functioning of informal consultations.

As already noted, the basic procedures for decision-making, as established by Art. IX of the WTO agreement, appear to be sound in view of the impact of WTO decisions on the rights and obligations of WTO members. However, there is a need to further reflect on the best consultation procedures to foster consensus in a manner which is transparent and participatory while ensuring effectiveness.

A large number of suggestions have been made on the organisation and functions of informal consultations, which remain an essential instrument for fostering consensus. A set of well researched guidelines are yet to be formulated in order to achieve this objective. Obviously, such guidelines should remain flexible since they would need to be adapted to the specific requirements of any individual consultation process. Drawing upon ideas presented by many WTO members and on the July Statement by the Chairman of the General Council, it was suggested that elements to be considered for such guidelines could include:

- The purpose of informal consultations should be to facilitate the process of building-up consensus and not to replace decision-making in the competent WTO bodies.
- Without prejudice to initiatives undertaken by individual WTO members, informal consultations may be initiated by the Chairman of a WTO body and/or the Director General (or one of his deputies). Members should be advised of the intention to initiate such consultations.
- Participation in informal meetings should be broadly representative of the WTO membership at different levels of development and reflect the breadth of substantive views on the issue being discussed. The Chairman of the WTO body or the DG (DDG's) has particular responsibility to ensure adequate representation in the meeting.
- The results of such informal consultations should be reported on a regular basis to the competent body concerned. Further informal consultations should take into account the views expressed in the open-ended meeting.

Recommendations of the European Commission on WTO Functioning

Apart from the issue of guidelines for informal consultations - on which a consensus can be rapidly reached

- the European Commission feels that further analysis of a number of other ideas be taken up to improve decision-making. In particular, following issues were suggested for further discussions:

- **The Feasibility of a Consultative Group**

A number of delegations have expressed interest in further discussing the possibility of establishing a consultative group (formal or informal) broadly representative of the WTO membership, but which could advise the Director General and, where appropriate, present recommendations to the General Council. A similar type of body (the Central Government 18) was in function between 1975 and 1988. A consultative group could contribute towards ensuring greater involvement of senior level capital based officials in the management of the WTO and foster open discussion on broad trends affecting the WTO System. Such a group would not, however, constitute an alternative to informal processes aimed at facilitating consensus on individual subjects, as discussed above.

- Decisions on Procedural Matters

Without prejudice to the need to maintain the overall principle of decision-making by consensus, consideration could be given to simplified procedures in relation to certain types of decision which do not affect the substantive rights and obligations of WTO members. The Director General could be asked to present a typology of different kinds of WTO decisions with a view to examine the opportunity of developing specific rules in respect to certain decisions.

- **Role of the Director-General**

The Director General does not have an expressly recognised right of initiative and normally acts on the basis of mandates specifically given by the membership. While maintaining the nature of the WTO as a member-driven organisation, there is a need to review the role of the Director General with a view to enhance his/her capacity to provide the members with independent, objective analysis and advice. The EC would be interested in further discussions on this issue.

2. Measures to foster the flow of information and participation by all members

An important objective of any effort to improve WTO functioning should be to facilitate the flow of information and effective participation by all WTO members and, in particular, those developing countries that do not have resident representatives in Geneva or only maintain small missions. The efforts by such countries to have a greater input in WTO process deserve the full support of other WTO members and the WTO Secretariat.

The efforts undertaken by the Director General and individual WTO members to involve non-resident representatives more fully in the work of the Organisation while avoiding duplication of initiatives are welcomed. The establishment of an ACP/Liaison office in Geneva should contribute towards this goal. Enhanced transparency in informal consultation processes would contribute towards more effective participation. There is, however, a need for targeted measures to facilitate participation by non-resident representatives and small developing country delegations. The Secretariat should develop particular efforts to facilitate the flow of information towards such countries. Moreover, their needs should be given particular priority in WTO technical assistance.

Effective participation by all members can also be promoted through measures to improve the management of WTO meetings. In this connection, the proposal by the African group to rationalise the scheduling, number and duration of meetings with a view, where appropriate, to having longer and less frequent meetings and to ensure better thematic co-ordination in establishing the calendar of meetings, deserves merit.

While some progress in the short term can be achieved through improved working methods and management of meetings, there is also merit in initiating a reflection on whether the current WTO committee structure could be further streamlined. For instance, consideration could be given to the possibility of merging a number of existing committees along functional lines rather than a situation in which each individual WTO agreement has a separate committee for its administration.

It should be noted, however, that such changes would imply amending existing WTO agreements. The Director General could also further study the scope for further streamlining of notification requirements, while maintaining overall transparency.

3. Measures to improve Ministerial meetings and the General Council

As regards improvements in the preparation and organisation of WTO Ministerials, a number of measures could be taken which, to a large extent, correspond to prior GATT/WTO practice:

(i) Both in the preparatory process and in the Ministerial itself, there has to be a proper combination of informal processes and meetings open to all WTO members.

(ii) There has to be a clear delineation between the role of the host country and that of the Director General. The role of the host country should be limited to chairing the plenary session, while informal processes should be handled by the DG, assisted by his DDG's.

(iii) The structure for negotiations must be set in advance of the Ministerial meeting and planning should imply that all necessary time is given to the actual negotiation of texts. Chairs of Working Groups should also be identified sufficiently in advance to allow for proper preparation. Where appropriate, sessions at senior official level should be held before the Ministerial starts.

Apart from the issue of improved preparation of Ministerial meetings, there is merit in considering the periodicity and functions of WTO Ministerials. Most international organisations - such as the Bretton Woods institutions or UN specialised agencies - hold yearly meetings at ministerial level. Political involvement and steering of the organisation could be enhanced if WTO Ministerial Conferences were also held on a yearly basis. Apart from decision making, Ministerial Conferences would also be expected to discuss a report on the activities of the WTO. This report could also highlight significant policy issues affecting the trading system.

Apart from improvements in WTO Ministerials, consideration could be given to means of enhancing the role of the General Council. The General Council should have overall responsibility for the coherent management and to supervise the activity of subsidiary bodies. Periodic meetings with the chairs of the main WTO bodies would contribute towards this goal. Moreover, the capacity of the Council to exercise an oversight role would be enhanced through a streamlining of the WTO Committee structure and improved procedures for decision making.

4. Enhanced External Transparency

In 1998, the EC presented proposals on derestriction of WTO documents and called for a review of existing WTO guidelines in order to strengthen procedures for consultation with NGO's. Since then, there has been considerable discussion of such issues in the General Council. The primary responsibility for dialogue with civil society falls at the level of each WTO member. However, enhanced external transparency in WTO operations has an important facilitating role. Building upon the proposals presented so far, the EC supports the following steps to enhance external transparency:

- Ensure immediate derestriction of most WTO documents. With a few limited exceptions, it should be possible to provide for the immediate derestriction of working documents. Secretariat background papers, meeting minutes and agendas and panel reports once translated into all 3 official languages. The Secretariat could also be encouraged to increase further the user-friendliness of the WTO web-site on which the derestricted documents are published.
- Enhance contacts and exchange of information between the WTO Secretariat and NGO's, along the lines of existing initiatives.
- Ensure a more regular organisation of symposia and other forms of informal dialogue with civil society on a broader range of WTO issues.
- On a voluntary basis, meetings of the TPRM could be open to parliamentarians and NGO's of the country under

review. This would enhance public interest in the TPRM exercise and would provide an opportunity for stakeholders to be better aware of other countries concerns with the trade policies followed by the country under review.

- Hold an annual open meeting of the WTO. Such a meeting could be held at either ministerial or senior official level. Apart from the discussion of a report on WTO activities, a symposium could be organised for dialogue with civil society as well as discussion panels including the participation of the heads of other international organisations.
- Hold, on a yearly basis and back to back with the annual open WTO meeting, a meeting of parliamentarians of WTO members. Greater involvement of national parliaments in WTO activities would play an important role in fostering greater public understanding and support for the multilateral trading system. The establishment of a WTO Parliamentary Consultative Assembly, would provide a valuable forum for interparliamentary dialogue on the main subjects discussed in the WTO and should therefore be further pursued.

Apart from the measures above, a review could be initiated of existing WTO guidelines in order to strengthen procedures for consultations with NGO's. In this connection, consideration could be given to the possibility of establishing a formal accreditation system for NGO's. In this connection different systems of accreditation could be discussed, taking into account the experience of other international organisations.

5.9 Future Round of WTO Meetings: European Commission's Stand

EC convinced that fundamental reasons for a broad agenda, and which have lead the Council and the Parliament to rally behind the Commission's proposals, remain valid:

- EC wants to, and must, further liberalise access to markets for goods and services, on the basis of predictable and non-discriminatory rules;
- The WTO must update and improve its rules in response o globalisation;
- Developing countries must be much better integrated into the system and have freer market access;
- The general public continues to be concerned, indeed worried, by the impact of globalisation on the environment, health, social standards and cultural diversity.

Sustaining the momentum for a round

The priority is to stay on course and keep the position, which the European Union was able to demonstrate in Seattle, thanks to the fruitful co-operation between the Commission, Parliament and Council. EC should continue to promote actively its position, namely, the launch of a new round based on a broad agenda as soon as possible. It is nevertheless necessary to proceed with a certain degree of caution, as they cannot run the risk of a second unsuccessful attempt.

There are a number of urgent questions that should be addressed. These concern as short-term measures to restore confidence in the WTO system. First of all, it is necessary to address the questions which concerns developing countries, in particular the least developed countries, which are those, who feel most frustrated by the failure in Seattle. This must be accompanied by concrete measures in the field of capacity building and technical assistance, which should aim to improve developing countries' participation in WTO negotiations. A dialogue with these countries should also be envisaged on the issues surrounding implementation.

Moreover, there are still a number of other problems, which should have been resolved in Seattle, like the question of transitional periods in subsidy agreements, TRIPS, customs valuation and TRIMS. There is also the electronic commerce moratorium that expired at Seattle. All these issues need to be dealt with in the very near future.

Finally, as regards improving the institutional functioning of the WTO, EC is currently preparing proposals distinguishing between what it can do in the short term and what could be done in the longer term.

In the short term it would be possible to envisage a series of measures aimed at improving the organisation of ministerial conferences so as to facilitate the participation of developing countries and promote greater external transparency. For example, EC could improve the preparation and running of Ministerial Conferences and simplify the working procedures. One could envisage informal processes involving a representative number of WTO members at different stages of development.

In order to improve the organisation's external transparency, EC could consider strengthening its dialogue with civil society and better structuring it (e.g. through a formal accreditation system for NGOs at Geneva). It could also envisage an annual public meeting of the WTO to discuss the organisation's activities.

More far-reaching improvements to the WTO system, in the context of international governance, should be the subject of a longer-term review, possibly within the context of a new round of negotiations, or in parallel with them.

To facilitate this review exercise, the Commission believes it would be useful to consider setting up an expert working group charged with producing ideas and recommendations. Besides the above mentioned factors, following factors should also be looked into:

- A way of strengthening this contact in the immediate future would be to hold an annual meeting of members of parliament from the Member States of the WTO.
- At a later stage, the setting up of a consultative parliamentary assembly at the WTO could be envisaged, as has been suggested by parliamentarians from the WTO Member States present in Seattle.

5.10 Conclusions

Despite liberalisation of various policies and procedures, India has so far been unable to define its ability and direction to conduct international trade in the face of a highly competitive international business environment. The size and content of India's export basket has remained almost the same over the past four decades.

Under the WTO, non-tariff barriers will have to be encountered and, therefore, India should aim at discouraging their proliferation. India must quickly take decisions based on its national interests so as to minimise the adverse effects and maximise the opportunities arising out of GATT.

The past 50 years have seen an exceptional growth in world trade. Merchandise exports grew on average by 6 per cent annually. Total trade in 1997 was 14-times the level of 1950.

India is one of the major beneficiaries of the tariff reduction package as agreed upon in the Final Agreement. As a part of the current reform process which was initiated in July 1991, India has already brought down its duty level to 40 per cent in the short run and 20 per cent in the medium term. In case of capital goods imports, even this is reduced to 10-15 per cent under certain conditions.

GATT and the WTO have helped to create a strong and prosperous trading system contributing to unprecedented growth. As far as India is concerned, the implications are that in the short run, gains may be unimpressive, but certainly it will pick up in the long run as the reform process gathers momentum.

The EC is proposing an agenda for the round that is relevant to the 21st century and that can facilitate the economic development of all the members of the WTO. The momentum in favour of a round is picking up, though there still are challenges ahead. The developing countries have to be convinced that a new round will address their interests, and that they stand to gain far more from a round than from the continuation of the status quo. Also the EC must collaborate with developed countries and persuade the United States to lend its active support for a round that will have development concerns at its core.

The following issues seem to take on a major importance for the WTO work in the future as these points are being continuously stressed by the main trading partners, the EU, the USA, Canada and Japan: transparency in the work carried, trade and environment, trade and competition, social concerns including the adoption of core labour standards, the integration of the world's least developed countries into the WTO system and electronic commerce, which can be considered an important engine of economic growth in the 21st century.

An important point to be noted here is that there might be a new situation once China is in the WTO. Its accession is welcomed and is good for the WTO also, but it will make the conduct of a round more difficult. Also the business support for the WTO system is needed and for further liberalisation. The opponents of the WTO must not be allowed to gain the upper hand and win the public debate.

What matters in the end is that WTO must achieve the goal of continued free economic expansion and a strengthened rule-based system, reflecting the new economic realities of today's globalised world, in an effort to harness globalisation for sustainable development. This will be good for India, good tor the EU and good for the multilateral system from which we all benefit.

Chapter 6

Foreign Direct Investment in India: Developments and Future Prospects

6.1 Foreign Direct Investment: Theoretical Settings

Investment in a country by individuals and organisations from other countries is an important aspect of international finance. This flow of international finance may take the form of portfolio investment (acquisition of securities) or direct investment (creation of productive facilities).

Foreign Direct Investment (FDI) is the outcome of the mutual interests of multinational firms and host countries. FDI is generally defined as a form of long-term international capital movement, made for the purpose of productive activity and accompanied by the intention of managerial control or participation in the management of a foreign firm.

According to the International Monetary Fund, FDI is defined as "investment that is made to acquire a lasting interest in an enterprise operating in an economy other than that of the investor. The investor's purpose being to have an effective voice in the management of the enterprise"[1]. It should not be confused with portfolio investment, which does not seek management control, but is motivated by profit. Portfolio investment occurs when individual investors invest, mostly through stockbrokers, in stocks of foreign companies in foreign land in search of profit opportunities.

The essence of Foreign Direct Investment is the transmission to the host country of a package of capital, managerial, skill and technical knowledge. It is an investment made to acquire a lasting interest in foreign enterprise with the purpose of having an effective voice in its management. FDI may take the form of purchase of securities in a foreign corporation, existing or formed, for the purpose, but its essence is control. Control is sought for the purpose of squeezing all the rent, in a Ricardian sense, out of a given advantage, often one technology, sometimes is the capacity of a vertically integrated company, stretching across national boundaries, to co-ordinate separate stages of production and distribution more efficiently than the automatic competitive market can.

The wave of liberalisation and globalisation sweeping across the world has opened many national markets for international business. Global private investment, in most part, is now made by transnational corporations (TNCs) also referred to as multinational corporations (MNCs). Clearly, these transnational organisations play a major role in world trade and investments because of their demonstrated management skills, technology, financial resources and related advantages Recent developments in the global market are indicative of the rapidly growing international business (presently accounting for one-third of the total global output) in terms of both market size and geographical diversification [2]. The end of the twentieth century has already marked a tremendous growth of international investments, trade and financial transactions along with the integration and openness of international markets.

A recent United Nations report has revealed that FDI flows are less volatile than portfolio flows. To quote, "FDI flows to developing and transition economies in 1998 declined by about 5 per cent from the peak in 1997, a modest reduction in relation to the effects on other capital flows of the spread of the Asian financial crisis to global proportions. FDI flows are generally much less volatile than portfolio flows. The decline was modest in all regions, even in the Asian economies most affected by the financial crisis."[3].

6.1.1 Significance of FDI

FDI provides financial resources for investment in the host country and thereby augments the domestic saving efforts. This contribution of FDI is, however, small for most developing countries. Thus, the share of FDI in gross domestic investment in developing countries was only 3.2 percent in 1992 and the relevant ratio for some countries of the Asian region (e.g. Korea and India) was even less than one percent. On the other hand, there are some countries in which the contribution of FDI to domestic capital formation has been significant. For example, the ratio of FDI to gross domestic capital formation in Thailand, Singapore and Hong Kong were 6.3 percent, 29.4 percent and 12.1. percent respectively, during the period 1986 to 1991.

Another contribution of FDI is that it provides the much needed foreign exchange to help bridge the balance of trade deficit. Indeed, in the wake of the debt crisis, FDI has come to be viewed as an increasingly important source of external finance for developing countries.

A much more important contribution of FDI lies in raising the technological standards and levels of efficiency and competitiveness of the host country. This can occur in several ways. FDI brings with it complementary assets such as technology, management and organisational competence and there are spill-over effects of these assets on the rest of the economy. As the foreign-owned enterprise comes into competition with the local firms, the latter category of enterprises are forced to improve their technology and standards of product quality. Further, the foreign-owned enterprises pressurises and assists the local related and support industries to improve the quality of their products and ensure greater reliability of delivery, both of which make it necessary for the related and support industries to upgrade their technology.

Another benefit of FDI is that it helps the host country improve its export performance. By raising the level of efficiency and the standards of product quality, FDI makes a positive impact on the host country's export competitiveness. Further, because of the international linkages of transnational corporations (TNCs), FDI provides to the host country better access to foreign markets. Also, where the foreign investment has been made with the specific intention of sourcing parts/components (or even final products) from the host country to take advantage of low cost conditions there (e.g. low wages), FDI contributes to exports directly.

It is needless to add here that enhanced export possibility contributes to the growth of the host economies by relaxing demand side constraints on growth. This is especially important for those countries which have a small domestic market and must increase exports vigorously to maintain their tempo of economic growth.

In judging the significance of FDI, especially from the viewpoint of developing countries, it is useful to make a distinction between macro-economic and micro-economic effects. The former is connected with issues of domestic capital formation, balance of payments, and taking advantage of external markets for achieving faster growth, while the latter is connected with the issues of cost reduction, product quality improvement, making changes in industrial structure and developing global inter-firm linkages.

In this context, it needs to be recognised that FDI is an aggregate entity, the sum total of the investments made by many diverse multinationals, each with its own corporate strategy. The micro-economic effects of the investment made by one multinational may be quite different from that of another multinational even if the investments are made in the same industry. Also, what benefits the local economy will be able to reap from the investments depends among other factors on the capabilities of the host country in regard to technology transfer and industrial restructuring.

6.1.2 Theories of FDI

The theories of FDI assert that the basis for such investment lies in transactions cost of transferring technical and other knowledge, and market imperfections. Needless to say that in a world of perfect markets, the multinational enterprises (MNEs) would not exist and there would be no FDI.

According to the Hymer-Kindleberger theory (Kindleberger, 1969), the foreign-owned firm would make an investment in the host country only if it possesses some compensating advantage which allows it to compete on equal terms with indigénous firms. This is, however, not a sufficient condition for FDI since the firm has the option of licensing the advantage (technology) to an indigenous producer or exporting the product to the host country. Clearly, certain other conditions have to be satisfied for FDI to arise. Three such conditions are: (a) the advantage is internally transferable (it can be exploited by a subsidiary of the parent firm without any additional cost to the parent firm or to the subsidiaries already exploiting it), (b) it is more profitable for the foreign-owned firm to exploit the advantage itself than to license it to an indigenous producer (because of imperfections in the market for knowledge and heavy firm to firm transfer costs of the advantage), and (c) exporting the product to the host country is not possible or unprofitable due to tariff or transport cost barriers.

A more general theory of TNCs traces their emergence to internalisation of markets (Buckley and Casson, 1991). The theory is based on three simple postulates; (1) firms maximise profits in a world of imperfect markets; (2) when markets in intermediate products are imperfect there is an incentive to bypass them by creating internal markets (within the firm); (3) internalisation of markets across national boundaries generates MNEs. It is argued that the location strategy of a vertically integrated firm is determined mainly by the interplay of comparative advantage, barriers to trade and regional incentives to internalise; the firm will be multinational whenever these factors make it optimal to locate different stages of production in different countries.

Another prediction of this theory is that unless either transport costs are very low, returns to scale at the plant level are high, or the comparative advantage of one location is very significant, the international acquisition and exploitation of knowledge will normally involve international production through a world-wide network of basically similar plants. Following this theory, one can see an important difference between the MNEs operating in the early part of this century and those which emerged in the later part of the century. It is argued that prior to the Second World War multinationality was a by-product of the internalisation of intermediate product markets in multistage production process, and in the post-war period it is a by-product of internalisation of markets in knowledge.

The two theories discussed above seek to explain FDI without making a distinction with regard to the country of origin. Kojima has argued that there is an inherent difference between FDI originating in the West and that in Japan (Kojima, 1978). He has developed a theoretical framework which integrates trade theory with FDI. This framework makes it possible for him to contrast 'Japanese type" foreign investment with 'American type'. The theoretical framework brings out that the 'American type' FDI eliminates the basis for trade. In the Japanese case, on the other hand, the host country's production frontier expands in such a direction that the industries having comparative advantage expand while those having disadvantage contract, thus enhancing the basis for trade.

It is argued that Japanese FDI represents a search for location specific inputs to complement the skills developed by Japanese enterprises, and this makes it different from the FDI originating in the West.

It should be pointed out here that the 'Kojima theory' was developed in the first or early wave of Japanese FDI in the 1960s and 1970s. The features of Japanese FDI on which Kojima built his theory has changed fundamentally since the 1980s - in terms of technology, marketing and management skills which have got closer to American FDI. Thus, questions can be raised on the applicability of 'Kojima theory' to Japanese FDI of recent years.

Dunning's eclectic theory of international production (Dunning, 1988) explains both the ways in which overseas markets are served by enterprises of different nationalities and the industrial and geographical composition of such activities. According to this theory, a firm will make a direct investment in a foreign country if the following three conditions are satisfied: (1) it possesses some ownership advantages vis-à-vis firms of other nationality in serving particular markets; (2) it is more beneficial for the firm to use the advantages itself than to sell or lease them to foreign firms, and (3) it is profitable for the enterprise to utilise these advantages in conjunction with at least some factor inputs outside the home country. The greater the ownership advantage of the enterprise, the more the incentive to exploit these themselves. The more the economies of production and marketing favour a foreign location, the greater is the inducement for FDI.

The eclectic theory suggests that all forms of international production can be explained by reference to the above conditions. Location specific or country specific advantages have an important bearing on FDI; such advantages of particular host countries make FDI in them preferable to not only other potential host countries, but also domestic investment. It needs to be recognised further that an important determinant of FDI is the ability of the firm to generate ownership advantages which are best exploited by the firm in a foreign rather than in a domestic location. In this way, the eclectic theory is able to provide an explanation for differences in the industrial pattern of outward FDI of different industrialised countries.

While the eclectic theory provides a good explanation for the decisions of firms to invest abroad, it seems to us that the theory does not cover the competitive FDI induced by trade restrictions. When a country imposes restrictions on imports of a particular industrial product, there is obviously inducement to multinational firms of the industry to invest in that country. If one or two firms invest, the others must also do so to counter competition and ensure their market share even if the returns to investment are negligible or negative, particularly for late entrants. Some FDI in the US and Europe are of this variety. Also, multinationals may enter a market today even if it is not profitable to do so, because they foresee the future growth and want to have the first entrant's advantage.

6.1.3 Favourable Effects of FDI

Private foreign investment, mostly by multinational corporations, is an important form of international flow of financial resources. According to UNCTAD, "Of about $ 2,000 billion of net capital inflow in developing countries during 1990-1998, more than $ 700 billion have been direct investment"[4]. Foreign investment takes place for private gain but it has the following potential benefits for least developed countries (LDCs).

1. Foreign investment can fill the gap between desired investment and locally mobilised savings. Local capital markets are often not well developed. Thus, they cannot meet the capital requirements for large investment projects. Besides, access to the hard currency needed to purchase investment goods not available locally can be difficult. FDI solves both these problems at once as it is a direct source of external capital. It can fill the gap between desired foreign exchange requirements and those derived from net export earnings.

2. Foreign investment can supply a package of needed resources such as management experience, entrepreneurial abilities, organisational and technological skills. Foreign investment brings with it technological knowledge while

transferring machinery and equipment to developing countries. Production units in developing countries use outdated equipment and techniques that can reduce the productivity of workers and lead to the production of goods of a lower standard. The ability of domestic producers to compete abroad for export markets is reduced which, in turn, contributes to the difficulties of the developing countries to earn hard currencies. FDI can solve this problem because investment goods generally embody advanced technology.

3. Foreign investment can create employment in the modern sectors of developing countries.

4. It can benefit consumers in LDCs through lower prices/improved quality of goods and through new products.

5. Foreign investment can stimulate domestic investment through forward and backward linkages. For example, output of a foreign firm can be an input of domestic industries. Similarly, output of the domestic industries can be inputs for the foreign firms. If this is so, foreign firms create demand for industries producing goods purchased by them.

6.1.4 Potential Pitfalls of FDI

Foreign private investment is not an unmixed blessing. Governments of LDCs have to be very careful while deciding the magnitude, pattern and conditions of private foreign investment. The adverse implications of foreign investment are the following:

1. When foreign investment is competitive with home investment, the profits in domestic industries fall, leading to fall in domestic savings.

2. Contribution of foreign firms to public revenue through corporate taxes is considerably less because of

liberal tax concessions, excessive investment allowances, disguised public subsidies and tariff protection provided by the host government.

3. Foreign firms reinforce dualistic socio-economic structure and increase income inequalities. They create a small number of highly paid modern sector executives. They divert resources away from priority sectors to the manufacture of sophisticated products for the consumption of local elite. As they are located in urban areas, they create imbalance between rural and urban opportunities, accelerating flow of rural population to urban areas.

4. Foreign firms stimulate inappropriate consumption patterns through excessive advertising and monopolistic/oligopolistic market power. The products made by multinationals for the domestic markets behind tariff walls are not necessarily low in price and high in quality. Their technology is generally capital-intensive which does not suit the needs of a labour-surplus economy.

5. Foreign firms are able to extract sizeable economic and political concessions from competing governments of LDCs. These concessions may take the form of excessive protection, tax rebates and investment allowances. Consequently, private profits of these companies may exceed social benefits.

6. Continuous outflow of profits is too large in many cases, putting pressure on foreign exchange reserves. Foreign investors are very particular about profit repatriation facilities.

6.1.5 Determinants of FDI

To understand the scale and direction of FDI flows, it is necessary to identify their major determinants. The paper examines the factors influencing the destination of investment, i.e. the host-country determinants.

6.1.5.1 Size of the Market: Large countries provide substantial markets where the consumer demand for certain goods has been largely unfilled to date. This potential has been a drawback for many of the initial foreign-owned operations in these countries. This explains the massive FDI flows which the large size of China's market has attracted since early 1980s. In many cases, the establishment of a low cost marketing operation represents the first step by a multinational into the market of the country. This establishes a presence in the market and provides important insights into the ways of doing business and possible opportunities in the country.

6.1.5.2 Uncertainty: In many countries, the institutions of government are still evolving and there are unsettled political questions. Companies are unwilling to contribute large amounts of capital into an environment where some of the basic political questions have not yet been resolved. David Holland and Jeffrey Owens have observed, "One of the greatest negative factors inhibiting FDI is the uncertainty that surrounds doing business in a region....It is for this reason that companies may establish small operations initially, in order to gather the necessary information for a full assessment of the risks and opportunities of doing business"[5].

6.1.5.3 Macroeconomic Environment: Instability in the level of prices and the exchange rate makes business planning difficult and increases the level of uncertainty. This increases the perceived risk of making investments and so adversely affects the inflow of FDI.

6.1.5.4 Legal and Regulatory Framework: The transition towards a market economy entails the establishment of a legal and regulatory framework that is compatible with private sector activities and the operation of foreign-owned companies. The areas of importance in this field include protection of property rights, ability to repatriate profits, and a free market for currency exchange. It is important that these rules and their related administrative procedures are transparent and easily comprehensible.

6.1.5.5 Access to Basic Inputs: FDI can be attracted by a country through the easy availability of factors of production. Many developing countries have large reserves of skilled and semi-skilled workers that are available for employment at wages significantly lower than in developed countries. This provides an opportunity for foreign firms to make investments in these countries to cater to the export market. Availability of natural resources such as oil and gas, minerals and forestry products also determine the extent of FDI.

6.2 Global Trends in FDI since the 1980s

There was a major spurt in FDI flows during the 1980s. In five years to 1989, the flow of net FDI worldwide rose at a rate of 29 percent per annum, three times as fast as world trade. This period also saw a major change in the pattern of FDI flows. During 1978-80, USA accounted for 41 percent of total FDI outflow of developed countries. During 1987-90, the share of USA was much lower at 13 percent. FDI flows from Europe as well as Japan were much larger than those from USA.

A study conducted by the United Nations in the mid-nineties observed that the stock of FDI had been growing at an unprecedented high rate. It increased at an annual average rate of 15 percent between 1985-1991 compared with the rate of 10 percent between 1980-85. Another important feature of the nineties was the decline in the importance of USA as an investor. On the other hand, Japan and Germany had gained in importance.

Developed countries accounted for 97 percent of the foreign direct investment outflows and 68 percent of inflows in 1992. The countries of European Union, japan and USA accounted for almost 70 percent of total inflows.

As far as the developing countries are concerned, the absolute volume of foreign direct inflows continues to increase. Their share in world flows had declined from 25 percent in the early 1980's to 17 percent in the late 1980s. In the year 1992, their share was estimated at 32 percent. Among the developing countries, there were considerable variations. In the year 1990, while the share of countries of Asia was 55 percent, the Latin American countries accounted for about 40 percent. The share of African countries was only 5 percent.

Ten large developing countries namely Argentina, Brazil, China, Indonesia, Malaysia, Mexico, Republic of Korea, Taiwan, Thailand and Venezuela accounted for almost 65 per cent of the inflows to developing countries in 1992. In the 1980s, FDI was concentrated within the Triad (The EU, Japan and the United States). However, in the 1990s, the FDI flows to devêloped countries declined, while those to developing countries increased in response to rapid economic growth and fewer restrictions.

The rapid increase in FDI has been accompanied by significant changes in the sectoral composition, from the primary sector and resource based manufacturing towards services and technology intensive industries. The share of FDI financed through new equity capital and inter company loans has been increasing, while the share of reinvested earnings has been declining. However, in terms of inflows reinvested earnings are a considerable larger component of FDI in developing countries than in developed countries. Even though the share of foreign assets controlled by the largest firms is still very high, the role of small and medium size enterprises is significant and growing. Though size is not an insurmountable barrier for FDI, such enterprises face constraints in the areas of management and capital accessibility.

With falling barriers to internationalisation, including cheaper transportation, communication and finance, these enterprises are internationalising their operations. In fact, in most economies these enterprises which form more than 90 percent of firms are key contributors to job, innovations and exports. Small and medium enterprises from Japan are increasingly investing in developing countries.

Another study conducted by the United Nations observed that after a two-year slow-down in outflows (from $ 232 billion in 1990 to $ 171 billion in 1992), FDI outflows began recovering in 1993, reaching $ 195 billion. On the inflow side, the US resumed its position as the largest host country, with its inflows reaching almost $32 billion in 1993. On the outflow side, the US had strengthened its position as the largest source of FDI, investing abroad a record $50 billion. In early 1990s, the UK had also regained its position as the largest home country in the European Union. Even during the FDI recession in the developed countries, flows into developing countries continued to increase.

In 1993, developing countries attracted a record $ 80 billion of FDI (40% of total), twice the amount of flows in 1991 and same as the level of total world inflows in 1986. FDI flows in 1993 were the largest component of net resource flows to developing countries, comprising one-third of the total.

The growth of FDI flows to developing countries is unevenly distributed among regions and groups of developing countries. Most FDI flows continue still to be concentrated in 10 to 15 host countries overwhelmingly in Asia and Latin America. South, East and Southeast Asia had experienced the fastest economic growth in the world, and had remained the largest host region, accounting for 57% of total developing country's FDI in 1992.

China became the largest host country in the developing world, accounting for nearly three-quarters of the increase in FDI flows into developing countries in 1992 and over half of the estimated increase in 1993. With $ 26 billion inflows it had become the second largest host country in the world in 1993, after the US.

Average investment flows into Latin America and the Caribbean during the early 1990s were more than twice as high as those during the 1980s. The least developed countries as a group had received little FDI, their share of total developing country inflows declined from an annual average of 2.1 percent in 1986-90 to 0.6 percent in 1992.

However, small markets with low growth rates, poor infrastructure, high indebtedness, slow progress in introducing market and private-sector oriented economic reforms and low levels of technological capabilities reduced their attractiveness to foreign investors.

The remarkable expansion of FDI flows to developing countries had belied the fear that the opening of Central and Eastern Europe and the efforts of the countries of that region to attract such investment would divert investment flows from developing countries. It is also important to draw attention to the growth in FDI outflow from developing countries, which increased from $ 9 billion in 1991 to $ 47 billion in 1995.

The Asian Newly Industrialising Economies (NIEs) have played an important role as suppliers of investment. In 1995, FDI outflows from the Republic of Korea, Taiwan and Singapore were $ 10.1 billion while these countries received $ 10.2 billion in FDI inflow in that year. Behind the FDI flows are the facts that domestically these countries are facing rising wages and a consequent weakening of their international competitiveness, and internationally they are being fast caught up by the nearby Association of Southeast Asian Nations (ASEAN) countries. They are accordingly being forced to aggressively invest abroad to ensure survival of their industries. At the same time, they have to attract foreign investment to attain a high tech orientation in their industries.

The study concluded that the most important factors making developing countries attractive to foreign investors were rapid economic growth, privatisation programmes open to foreign investors and the liberalisation of the FDI regulatory framework.

6.3 FDI in India: Policy Initiatives

From 1950 to 1985, India followed a very suspicious policy regarding foreign investments. However, the scenario has changed drastically during the post-1991 period.

6.3.1 India's Position in Global Context

On the eve of Independence in 1947, India was a country at a low level of development with high incidence of poverty and inequality. The land-labour ratio was quite adverse. The economy was stagnant because of lack of capital. During the century long direct British rule the inflow of capital was not commensurate with the poor capital endowment of the country when there were apparently no political constraints on inflow to India. The low per capita income restricted the market. Foreign Investment did take place but mainly to export oriented industries such as tea, jute, coal etc. Most of the profits were repatriated and not reinvested. Such investment could not have led to growth as the objective was exploitation of the natural resources.

Since the inception of centralised planning in 1951 till 1980, India followed a preventive policy regime with restrictions on investment of capital and import of capital goods by local as well as foreign firms. The policy restrictions persisting till mid-80s consisted mainly of the restrictions on new and existing Foreign Direct Investment through screening and preventive measures. This trend of restricted Foreign Direct Investment continued till late 1980s.

Since 1991, the Government of India has embarked on a liberalisation and economic reforms programme with a view to bring about rapid and substantial economic growth and move towards globalisation of the economy. The new policies have substantially relaxed restrictions on foreign investment, industrial licensing and foreign exchange. Capital market has been opened to foreign investment and banking sector controls have been eased. Reserve Bank of India's *Report on Currency and Finance* (1998-99) maintained, "The Government is committed to promoting increased flow of Foreign Direct Investment (FDI) for better technology, modernisation, exports and for providing products and services of international standards. Therefore, the policy of the Government has been aimed at encouraging foreign investment, particularly in core infrastructure sectors so as to supplement national efforts"[6].

As a part of major initiatives to attract foreign investment, measures have been initiated to enter into agreements to provide for promotion and protection of investment. India has become a Member of Multilateral Investment Guarantee Agency (MIGA). Full subscription and membership rights have become operative from January, 1994. As a consequence, all investments approved by Government are insured against expropriation/ nationalisation by MIGA. Bilateral Investment Promotion and Protection Agreements have been signed with 46 countries including principal FDI investors such as the UK, Germany, Malaysia and Denmark. Others are in the process of being finalised.

6.3.2 Creating Congenial Environment for FDI

In order to attract foreign investment and to promote domestic entrepreneurial private activities, the Government of Prime Minister Mr. Narasimha Rao announced a new industrial policy in the Indian Parliament on July 24, 1991. The new policy introduced radical changes "to unshackle the Indian industrial economy from the cobwebs of unnecessary bureaucratic controls". Some of the provisions of the new policy, which have already proved to be a watershed in the post-Independence history of India, are the following:

6.3.2.1 Industrial Policy Reforms: The 1991 Industrial Policy abolished industrial licenses for all projects, except for a short list of 18 specified industries related to security and strategic areas, social reasons, hazardous chemicals, environmental reasons, and items of elitist consumption.

After further pruning of the list, presently there are only six industries under compulsory industrial licensing. These are: 1. Distillation and brewing of alcoholic drinks. 2. Cigars and cigarettes of tobacco and manufactured tobacco substitute. 3. Electronic aerospace and defence equipment, all types. 4. Industrial explosives including detonating fuses, safety fuses, gunpowder, nitro-cellulose and matches. 5. Hazardous chemicals. 6. Drugs and pharmaceuticals (bulk drugs industry has been delicensed) [7].

The new industrial policy removed the asset limits for MRTP totally. The MRTP Act is now used for controlling and regulating monopolistic, restrictive, and unfair trade practices. The MRTP Commission was given powers to initiate investigations suo moto or on complaints received from individual consumers or classes of consumers about monopolistic, restrictive, and unfair trade practices.

It raised the limit for foreign equity holding from 40 per cent to 51 per cent. The automatic clearance for direct foreign investment up to 51 per cent in high priority areas was a clear signal that the foreign investment was welcome. The new policy also announced automatic permission for foreign technology agreements in high priority industries. Moreover, the policy made liberal provisions for hiring foreign technicians, and foreign testing of indigenously developed technology.

With a view to raise resources and ensure wider participation, the new policy announced disinvestment in public sector undertakings in favour of mutual funds, financial institutions, workers, and the general public. While reservation of industries for the public sector was retained, there would be no bar for opening such areas to the private sector selectively.

The July 1991 policy statement reduced the list of industries reserved for public sector from 17 included in the Industrial Policy Resolution of 1956 to only 8. Subsequently, 4 more items were dereserved. Thus, at present there are only four industries reserved for the public sector. These are: 1. Arms and ammunition and allied items of defence equipment, defence aircraft and warships. 2. Atomic energy. 3. The substances specified in the schedule to the Notification Number S.O. 212 (E) dated March 15, 1995 of the Government of India in the Department of Atomic Energy. 4. Railway transport [8].

6.3.2.2 Financial Sector Reforms: Considering the strategic importance of the financial sector, the Government set up a Committee on Financial System in 1991 under the chairmanship of Mr. M. Narasimham. It was asked to examine all aspects relating to the structure, organisation, functions and procedures of the financial system. The Committee submitted its report in November 1991.

Based on the recommendations of the Narasimham Committee Report, banking sector has been opened for the private sector and presently ten private banks are in business. Joint ventures in banking have also been permitted.

An efficient capital market is an important constituent of a sound financial system. Efforts have been made to set up an effective regulatory framework covering major participants in the capital market. Similarly, the technology of trading and settlements in the stock exchanges has been upgraded. The Securities and Exchange Board of India (SEBI) has permitted internet-based securities trading. Foreign institutional investors and pension funds were allowed to enter the Indian stock market from 1993 onwards.

Life insurance business in India was nationalised in 1956 and since then the public sector Life Insurance Corporation has enjoyed monopoly in this field. People in general have all along been grumbling against LIC's monopolistic exploitation, poor service and high premium rates. Same was the case with general insurance business which was also monopolised by the Government. The public sector monopoly of insurance business was ended with the enactment of the Insurance Regulatory and Development Act, 1999. The insurance sector is now open to private sector participants and it can be expected that service to the consumer will improve.

6.3.2.3 Tax Reforms: In August 1991, the Government of India constituted a Tax Reforms Committee (TRC) to recommend a comprehensive reform of both direct and indirect tax laws. The Report of the Committee contained recommendations for restructuring and rationalisation of personal income tax, corporate income tax, wealth tax, excise duties, import tariff, tax administration and enforcement machinery. Based on the overall direction prescribed by the TRC, tax reforms introduced by the Government since mid-1991 are geared "to build a structure which is simple, relies on moderate tax rates but with a wider base and better enforcement" [9].

6.3.2.4 External Sector Reforms: Prior to mid-1991, foreign trade of India suffered from strict bureaucratic and discretionary controls. However, the new Government which took over at the Centre in June 1991 soon realised that

India's foreign trade policy must respond to the changes (liberalisation and openness) sweeping across the world. To reduce controls, simplify procedures and to create a congenial environment for trade, the Government made a Statement on Trade Policy in Parliament on August 13, 1991, ushering a new era in the foreign trade policy of India. Instead of controls and regulations, the focus shifted to promotion and development of foreign trade.

In India, about 99 per cent of customs revenue is derived from import duties which are levied on a wide range of commodities. Radical reforms have been introduced in the Indian customs tariff between 1991 and 2000. These reforms were necessary because the customs tariff had become, over the years, very complicated in terms of multiple rates, innumerable exemptions, excessive controls, and elaborate procedures. These infirmities of the customs tariff often led to delays, harassment, corruption, and litigation. Moreover, rationalisation and simplification of the customs duties was needed to move towards a market economy, freedom of trade, and opening up the Indian economy to the outside world.

With the liberalisation of foreign trade, exchange rate has assumed added significance. Presently, there is almost full convertibility on the current account and partial convertibility on the capital account. By and large, a floating exchange rate regime has been introduced. However, Government agencies do intervene occasionally to soften excessive fluctuations in currency rates.

As a part of India's external economy policy, capital account convertibility has remained a controversial issue for quite sometime. Justifiably, Indian Government has been very cautious in this regard, particularly after the disastrous experience of some East Asian Countries. It is true that globalisation has led to financial integration in world markets and presently large amounts of capital move freely across countries. However, volatility of these flows must be properly understood before taking decisions regarding convertibility of capital account. India has successfully avoided the trap so far and policymakers must remain cautious as regards capital account convertibility [10].

6.3.3 Routes for FDI Flow

FDI can be approved either through the Automatic Route or by the Government.

6.3.3.1 Automatic Route: Companies proposing foreign investment under the automatic route do not require any government approval, provided the proposed foreign equity is within the specified ceiling and the requisite documents are filed with the Reserve Bank of India (RBI) within 30 days of receipt of funds. The automatic route encompasses all proposals:

(a) where the foreign investment in the equity capital of the Indian Company is up to 50/51/74/100 per cent as the case may be as applicable to the list of high priority industries/items given in Annexure III [11], and

(b) where the proposed items(s) of manufacture/activity does not require an Industrial Licence and is not reserved for the Small Scale Sector.

The above is also applicable for existing companies wishing to raise foreign equity up to 50/51/74/100 per cent, as the case may be. If the equity is proposed as part of an expansion programme, the expansion programme must be in the high priority industries listed in Annexure III. When the increase in equity is not proposed for purposes of an expansion, the company must be pre-dominantly engaged in the high priority industries listed in Annexure 3.

The automatic route for FDI and /or technology collaboration would not be available to those who have or had any previous joint venture on technology transfer /trade mark agreement in the same or allied field in India.

6.3.3.2 Government Approval: For the following categories, government approval for FDI though the FIPB would be necessary:

(a) proposals attracting compulsory licensing.

(b) items of manufacture reserved for the small scale sector

(c) acquisition of existing shares

(d) foreign investment proposals where the parameters for automatic approval are not met and the company has to notify the same to SIA (Secretariat for Industrial Assistance) within 30 days of receipt of funds as also allotment of shares.

(e) in case of infusion of foreign equity by a company without changing the percentage of equity that has already been approved by the Government and where the original project cost was up to Rs. 600 crore, no prior approval of FIPB/ Government is required. The company has to notify the same to SIA within 30 days of receipt of funds as also allotment of shares.

6.3.3.3 Foreign Investment Promotion Board (FIPB): The FIPB is especially empowered to engage in purposive negotiation and also consider proposals in totality free from predetermined parameters on procedures. Industry Secretary is the Chairman of FIPB. The Finance Secretary, Commerce Secretary and Secretary(Economic Relations) Ministry of External Affairs are the other members of the FIPB.

The approach of FIPB is liberal for all sectors and all types of proposals. The totality of package proposed is examined and approved on merits within a period of thirty days. RBI has granted general permission under Foreign Exchange Regulation Act (FERA) in respect of proposals approved by the Government. Indian companies getting foreign investment approval through FIPB route do not require any further clearance from RBI for the purpose of receiving inward remittance and issue of shares to the foreign investors. Such companies are, however, required to notify the Regional Office concerned of the RBI of receipt of inward remittances within 30 days of such receipt and to file the required document with the concerned Regional Offices of the RBI within 30 days after issue of shares to the foreign investors.

6.3.3.4 Foreign Investment Promotion Council: The Government has recently constituted a Foreign Investment Promotion Council (FIPC) in the Ministry of Industry. It has been set up to have more target oriented approach towards foreign direct investment promotion. Its functions are to identify the sector/project within the country requiring foreign direct investment and target specific regions/counties of the world from where FDI will be brought through.

The relative importance of different channels of entry of FDI flows into the country can be seen from Table 6.1.

The automatic approval route of the RBI was introduced to facilitate FDI inflows. However, during the post-policy period , the actual investment flows through the automatic route of the RBI against total FDI flows has been quite insignificant. While FDI flows through the automatic route

Table 6.1: FDI Inflows in India by Different Categories: 1991 to 2001

(US $ million)

DIRECT INVESTMENT	1992-93	1994-95	1995-96	1996-97	1997-98	1998-99	1999-00	2000-2001#
1. RBI automatic route	42	171	169	135	202	179	171	330
2. SIA/FIPB route	222	701	1249	1922	2754	1821	1410	1262
3. NRI schemes	51	442	715	639	241	62	84	51
4. Acquisition of shares *	-	-	11	125	380	400	490	273
Total	**315**	**1314**	**2144**	**2821**	**3557**	**2462**	**2155**	**1916**

Source: Government of India, Ministry of Finance, *Economic Survey*, 2000-2001, p.118, Table 6.8.

* Relates to acquistion of shares of Indian companies by non-residents under Section 29 of FERA

\# Provisional for the months April-December.

accounted for 15.18% of the total FDI inflows in 1993-94, its share has declined since then and was only 8.68% in 1998-99. This is partly due to the fact that crucial areas like electronics, services and minerals are left out of the automatic approval route. Another limitation has been the ceiling of 51% on foreign equity holding. An increasing number of proposals were cleared through the FIPB route while the automatic approval route has been declining in the relative importance since 1994.

6.4 India's Share in FDI Flows to Developing Countries

Available data suggest that the share of India in FDI flows to developing countries is meagre. In 1998, India accounted for 1.2 per cent (2,258 million US$ out of 183,449 million US$) of total FDI flows to developing countries (Table 6.2).

As per Economic Survey 2000-2001, in terms of aggregate annual inflows, FDI maintained its declining trend for the second successive year after 1997-98. FDI inflows in India for the year 1999-2000 (US $ 2155 million) were lower than the pervious year (US $ 2462 million). Inflows in the current year 2000-2001, however, are showing signs of improvement. During April-December, aggregate FDI inflows have been higher (US $ 1916 million) than the comparable period of 1999-2000.

Despite progressively declining volumes of inflows, Mauritius and the US continue to be the largest sources of FDI for India. Apart from these two countries, Japan, Italy and Netherlands respectively were the other three major contributors during 1999-2000.

Table 6.2: FDI Flows to Developing Countries in 1998
(US $ million)

S. No.	Country	FDI flow	Per cent of total
1.	China	45,460	24.8
2.	Brazil	28,718	15.7
3.	Mexico	10,238	5.6
4.	Thailand	6,969	3.8
5.	Argentina	5,697	3.1
6.	Korea	5,143	2.8
7.	Poland	5,129	2.8
8.	Chile	4,792	2.6
9.	Venezuela	3,737	2.0
10.	Malaysia	3,727	2.0
11.	Colombia	2,983	1.6
12.	Czech Republic	2,540	1.4
13.	**India**	**2,258**	**1.2**

Source: Reserve Bank of India, *Report on Currency and Finance*, 1998-99, p.X-11.

While the growth of FDI inflows to India has been fairly satisfactory, India's share in the global FDI regime is still minuscule.

6.4.1 Reasons for Low Flows

According to a recent study, "India's neighbours that are relying heavily on FDI, such as China, Indonesia, Malaysia, and Thailand, have been pulling far ahead in economic growth, income levels, and productivity, while also increasing their security and geopolitical influence.

However, as per Economic Survey 2000-2001, the inflow of FDI to developing countries has been progressively increasing through the decade of 1990s. China continues to be the largest absorber of FDI among developing nations. Among the Southeast Asian economies, FDI inflows have sharply declined in Indonesia and Malaysia. The Republic of Korea has however, has experienced rapid jump in volume of FDI inflows in 1998 and 1999. As far as India is concerned, its share in total FDI flows to developing countries has declined by one percentage point from 1997 to 1999. The falling share is a cause for concern and underlines the need for even greater policy reforms in the FDI regime.

India's continuing ambivalence on FDI, as a result, exacts a heavy toll on the economy. Undoubtedly, India is ceding billions of dollars of FDI to its neighbours each year. While China achieved actual FDI inflows of around $ 45.3 billion in 1997, India settled for a mere $3.2 billion"[12].

The reasons for low inflows are attributable to a host of factors such as procedural disputes regarding land availability, environmental clearance, delays at State level in getting power and other infrastructural back up. These bottlenecks result in delays in the commencement of many projects. Moreover, sizeable investment flows are concentrated in the infrastructure industries, like power, refineries, telecom etc. where gestation period is long and projects take time to materialise.

6.4.2 Approvals and Actual Inflows

In a direct response to the liberal policy measures introduced by the Government since 1991, foreign direct investment in India has increased progressively in the post reform period both in terms of approvals and actual inflows. Table 6.3 shows the trends in approvals of FDI proposals vis-à-vis inflows. Approvals of foreign investment increased from US$ 325 million in 1991 to US$ 6,975 million in 1998. They aggregated to a total of US$ 55,111 million in the post liberalisation period, i.e. 1991 to 1998.

The actual inflow of foreign direct investment increased from US$ 155 million in 1991 to US$ 2,230 million in 1998. Cumulative inflows up to 1998 amounted to US$ 11,963 million. Actual inflows as a proportion of approvals have ranged between 13% to 22%. This proportion improved from 13.1% in 1992 to 32% in 1998.

6.5 Conclusion

Trade and finance are essential to integrate international markets which enable firms in one country to reach markets in another which usually and mostly result into foreign direct investment. Hence, the barriers to FDI are to be lowered.

In the decades of the eighties foreign investment policy had played a very limited role in the process of growth and

Table 6.3: FDI in India: Approvals and Actual Inflows

	1991	1992	1993	1994	1995	1996	1997	1998
Approvals								
Rs. crore	739	5256	11189	13590	37489	39453	57149	28783
US$ million	325	1781	3559	4332	11245	11142	15752	6975
Actual Inflows								
Rs. crore	351	675	1786	3009	6720	8431	12085	9116
US$ million	155	233	574	958	2100	2383	3330	2230
Actual flows as % of approvals (in US $ terms)	47.7	13.1	16.1	22.1	18.7	21.4	21.1	32.0

Source: Government of India, Ministry of Finance, *Economic Survey,* 1999-2000, p. 101, Table 6.8.

development. During the period 1986-90, there had been Rs. 900 crore worth origin direct investment flow to India which came to Rs. 180 crore per annum. This reveals that during the decade of eighties, India followed a restrictive foreign investment policy. From July 1991 onwards, Government of India, initiated a more liberal and productive foreign investment policy so that more and more foreign direct investment could be attracted and utilised for rapid industrial growth. Under the new foreign investment policy there has been a automatic approval of FDI upto 51 percent equity holding in 34 specified high priority, capital intensive, high tech units.

A special board known as Foreign Investment Promotion Board was also established to look after the regulation and monitoring of large foreign investment projects where higher foreign equity limit of more than 51 percent may be allowed, keeping in mind interest of the nation. In 1991, investments in most areas of India's economy are reserved for the public sector. Now there is hardly a sector from which domestic or foreign private investors are excluded. This had made India a more attractive FDI destination, as is borne out by the inward FDI flows. FDI proposals worth a mere $ 167 million were approved in 1991; the figure rose to $ 14 billion in 1997.

The profile and pattern of foreign investments are now changing considerably both by sector and country of origin. Earlier, over 50 percent of the investment was in areas such as fuels, metallurgy and chemicals. There is now a distinct shift towards the infrastructure sectors such as power and telecom. The EU has emerged as India's largest investor in terms of actual inflows since 1994. In the post liberalisation period of 1991-96, the EU became the number one investor with $ 1053 million worth of actual FDI inflow into India, ahead of the USA ($ 753 million).

EU investments into India have shown an increasing trend, the compounded average annual growth rate for the EU being over 135 percent. Sectorally, the EU has a substantial financial stake in industrial machinery, transport, electrical goods and electronics, textiles, chemicals and consultancy.

Since 1994, there has been a spurt in investments in the infrastructure and automotive sectors. In addition, there is an increasing interest shown by the Europcan companies in the Indian food processing, horticulture and floriculture sectors. In 1997, FDI approvals showed a trend towards infrastructure with power accounting for 31 over 14 percent FDI.

According to Economic Survey 2000-2001, the engineering industry continues to attract the largest volume of FDI inflows. In 1999-2000, the sector experienced aggregate inflows worth US $ 326 million. Electronics and electrical equipment industries were the second largest recipient of FDI with aggregate inflows amounting to US $ 172 million. Food and dairy products had a sharp increase in FDI with inflows increasing from US $ 19 million in 1998-99 to US $ 121 million in 1999-2000. Another industry witnessing increase in FDI inflows during 1999-2000 was pharmaceuticals where aggregate FDI during the year rose to US $ 54 million compared to US $ 28 million in 1998-99.

Notes

1. International Monetary Fund, *Balance of Payments Manual*, Washington, DC, 1977, p.408.

2. Surendra Pradhan, "Foreign Direct Investment: Risk, Return and Host Country's Strategy", *Journal of Management Research*, September-December 2000, pp. 18-19.

3. United Nations, *World Economic and Social Survey*, 1999, p. 35.

4. United Nations Conference on Trade and Development, *Trade and Development Report*, 1999, p. 115.

5. David Holland and Jeffrey Owens, "Taxation and Foreign Direct Investment: The Experience of the Economies in Transition", *Bulletin for International Fiscal Documentation*, February 1996, p. 48.

6. Reserve Bank of India, *Report on Currency and Finance*, 1998-99, p. IV-8.

7. *Ibid*., p. IV-8.

8. *Ibid*., p. IV-8.

9. Government of India, Ministry of Finance, Budget Papers, 1995-96, *Speech of the Finance Minister*, Part B, p. 17.

10. It is noteworthy that East Asian crisis was not the result of liberalised foreign trade policies and foreign direct investments. It was clearly attributable to unbridled short-term capital inflows.

11. For a detailed list of high priority industries, see Annexure III of the Industrial Policy Statement (July 24, 1991) of the Government of India.

12. Nirupam Bajpai and Jeffrey D. Sachs, Foreign Direct Investment in India - I, *The Hindu*, June 30, 2000.

Chapter 7

Foreign Investment in India: A Sectoral Analysis

The Indian Government has placed special emphasis on drawing foreign investment into sectors which are perceived of high priority for the following reasons:

1. Need for rapid development.
2. Volume of investment required.
3. Importance for overall economic growth and employment.
4. Comparative advantages in terms of human or natural resources.

Table 7.1 indicates the industry-wise break-up of FDI flows from January 1991 to December 2000. The Table includes only some of the promising sectors in which the FDI approvals have been substantial in the past or which offer good potential for future investments.

Industry-wise break up of the FDI flows from January 1991 to December 2000 indicates that the bulk of the foreign investment has been in the priority sector.

Telecommunications and power have accounted for 33.26 % of total approvals. Food processing and metallurgical industries have accounted for another 9.38 %. Transportation industry, electrical equipment and services have taken up another 23.62 % of the total approvals.

The sectoral composition of FDI approvals reveal that they can be broken up into three major compartments:

Special policy thrust and/or attractive incentives attract 41.18% :

Table 7.1: Sector Wise Break-up of Foreign Direct Investment and Technical Collaboration Approved During the Period from 1.8.1991 to 31.12.2000

(in Rs. million)

S.No.	Name of industry	No. of approvals			Amount of FDI approved	% of total amount of FDI approved
		Total	Technical	Financial		
1.	**Fuels**					
	Power	227	17	210	361743.88	14.66
	Oil refinery	239	111	128	195298.57	7.92
	Power (other)	70	6	64	53111.38	2.15
	Oil refinery (oth.)	108	62	46	45845.57	1.86
	Others (fuels)	148	55	93	36189.41	1.47
	Total	792	251	541	692188.81	28.06

2. Telecommunications					
Telecommunications	340	100	240	90082.42	3.65
Radio paging	50	4	46	12308.95	0.50
Cellular mobile/ Basic Telephone service	185	10	175	268646.35	11.90
Telecommunications (I & B)	100	3	97	80298.78	3.25
Others	23	2	21	7508.53	0.30
Total	698	119	579	458845.03	18.60
3. Service Sector					
Financial	357	8	349	104390.51	4.23
Non-financial services	322	20	302	31252.33	1.27
Banking services	25	0	25	1819.27	0.07
Hospital and diagnostic centres	88	13	75	6532.20	0.26
Other (services)	45	6	39	8394.69	0.34
Total	837	47	790	152389.00	6.18

4. Food Processing Industries					
Food products	698	130	568	86530.00	3.51
Marine products	92	20	72	921.76	0.04
Miscellaneous	8	0	8	123.17	0.00
Total	798	150	648	87547.92	3.55
5. Transportation industry					
Automobile industry	727	398	329	43128.19	1.75
Air/Sea transport	169	17	152	27835.16	1.13
Passenger cars	57	5	52	72001.96	2.92
Auto ancillaries	182	86	96	20699.13	0.84
Ports	16	0	16	12494.50	0.51
Others	109	32	77	8308.68	0.34
Total	1260	538	722	184467.61	7.48

6. Hotels and Tourism					
Hotel and restaurants	356	127	229	36116.46	1.46
Tourism	79	17	62	7827.44	0.32
Others	14	3	11	2557.18	0.10
Total	449	147	302	46501.08	1.88
7. Metallurgy					
Ferrous	365	216	149	73760.21	2.99
Non-ferrous	63	30	33	7718.62	0.31
Special alloys	84	52	32	8485.60	0.34
Mining service	54	13	41	41922.58	1.71
Misc. (Other items)	77	28	49	11909. 91	0.48
Total	643	339	304	143796.77	5.83

8. Electronics					
Electrical equipment	1560	864	696	55926.82	2.27
Computer software industry	1551	79	1472	159591.24	6.47
Electronics	441	148	293	29400.97	1.19
Computer hardware	3	0	3	9.04	0.00
Others	44	17	27	863.47	0.04
Total	3599	1108	2491	245791.54	9.96

Source: SIA (*Secretariat for Industrial Assistance*) Newsletter, 01/2001, Government of India, New Delhi.

Telecommunications 18.60 %
Power 14.66 %
Oil refining 7.92 %
Potential for high growth areas attract 26 %
Automobiles and transportation 7.48 %
Services 6.18 %
Electronics software and electrical equipment 9.96 %
Hotels and tourism 1.88 %
Natural resource advantages draw 9.38 %
Metallurgical Industries 5.83 %
Food Processing 3.55 %

The particular industrial sectors which have been identified as presenting tremendous opportunities for foreign investments are: power; hydrocarbons; telecommunications; electronics; mining & metallurgy; roads and highways; ports; tourism; services; automobiles; drugs and pharmaceuticals; food processing; textiles; and insurance.

7.1 Power

The power sector is India's top infrastructure priority. Shortage of power has been cited as one main problem of the economy and it is realised that the future is bleak unless enough power is generated for industrial and consumer use. That is precisely why the government accords top priority to foreign investment in this capital-intensive sector.

The main elements of the policy of the Government regarding private investment in the power sector are the following:

1. Foreign investment in the power sector is actively encouraged and can take place either in the form of a joint venture with an Indian partner or as a fully-owned operation with 100% foreign equity. According to the new liberalised

policy, foreign equity up to 100% in the field of electricity generation, transmission and distribution except in atomic reactor power plants can be held by a company through automatic route. However, foreign equity in projects under this category should not exceed Rs.15 billion.

2. Companies may operate either as power distributor or generator companies.

3. Power generation companies are required to supply to State Electricity Boards (SEBs) who in turn will distribute the power.

4. Since the entry of private sector in the power generation, Central Electricity Authority (CEA) has accorded techno-economic clearance (TEC) to 56 private sector power projects amounting to around 28,849 MW [1].

5. A series of approvals are required for power projects. These include 'in principle' endorsement of a project followed by approvals of techno-feasibility reports, funding plans, clearance by environmental authorities, Foreign Investment Promotion Board etc.

7.1.1 Prospects and Opportunities: This sector offers the following prospects and opportunities to the potential investors.

1. 100% foreign equity is permitted in this sector.

2. Private power projects are based on a 16-18 per cent return on equity, so their costs are high. Since they have to sell their power to the financially weak State Electricity Boards, there were concerns about whether the foreign investors would get their money back. To allay these fears, the Government provides guarantees to foreign investors in projects found viable.

According to *Economic Survey*, 1999-2000, "Issue of counter guarantee of Government of India has been approved on December 22,1999 for the Mangalore Thermal Power Project (1000 MW) of M/s. Cogentrix Energy Incidence. in Karnataka and to the lb Valley Thermal Power project (500 MW) of M/s. AES lb Valley Corp. in Orissa"[2].

3. The World Bank has advised that the State Electricity Boards be restructured into smaller units. The bank has also recommended creation of smaller units for privatisation. This has been done in Greater Noida in north Indian state of Uttar Pradesh and the general mood is to do the same in parts of the country. These developments have made foreign investors confident of investing in India.

4. Special incentive package including tax holiday, rationalised depreciation, reduced customs duty on equipment etc. has been devised.

5. A blend of thermal, hydel and nuclear sources of energy are available. Non-conventional energy from solar, wind and tidal sources are also encouraged.

7.2 Telecommunications

Telecommunications is a prime support service needed for rapid growth and modernisation. It is also one of the fastest growing sectors in India and has immense potential for growth. The telecommunication activity is commercial in nature and people are willing to pay for it. Abundant investment opportunities exist in areas of basic and cellular telephony, communication infrastructure, optic fibre cable, gateways, satellite based communications etc. The telecom sector has witnessed the presence of many leading foreign companies including US companies: AT&T, Motorola, US West, Hughes, Harris, Qualcomm, Sprint, Telstra, NTT, Singapore Telecom, Philippine Telecom, Bezeq, Siemens,

Ericsson, Nokia, Fujitsu, Alcatel, and Bell Canada among others.

In order to modernise the telecom facilities in the country, the Government has announced a comprehensive policy for attracting private, including foreign investment in Value Added and Basic Services.

7.2.1 Value Added Services: The value added services were thrown open to private sector in 1992. The value added services, where private, including foreign investment is encouraged include: electronic mail, voice mail, data services, audio text services, video text services etc.

In view of the constraints in the number of companies that can be allowed to operate, a policy of selection through a system of tendering is followed, for the following value added
services: radio paging, cellular mobile telephone, and Global Mobile Personal Communications by Satellite (GMPCs).

All foreign investment proposals in the above telecom services require licence from Department of Telecommunications (DOT) and approval of FIPB.

7.2.2 Basic Services: The private sector participation in the basic telecom services is guided by the National Telecom Policy, 1994. Basic services were opened to private participation in 1994 by dividing the country into 21 Telecom Circles and allowing one private operator per Circle to compete with DoT. Only companies registered in India will be permitted to participate in providing basic voice telephone services. In the case of a joint venture, foreign equity up to 49% would be permitted. However there will be no limit of foreign equity in the manufacturing sector. Six licences for basic services have been granted for six States. Two operators M/s. Bharati Telenet Ltd. in

Madhya Pradesh, and Hughes Ispat Ltd. in Maharashtra have started providing services [3].

The Telecom Regulatory Authority of India (TRAI) , an autonomous body, has been set up as a regulatory authority to set standards, regulate prices, ensure technical compatibility among different service providers, fix access charges, protect consumer interest and resolve disputes between service providers.

7.2.3 Prospects and Opportunities: 1. India has a mere 1.2 telephones for every 100 of its people. This is way below international standards and is not becoming of a country aspiring to be a major player in the global economy of the 21st century. This means that opportunities for investment in this sector are immense.

2. Basic voice services is the biggest market. As on 31.3 1997, the telecom network had 145.33 lakh Direct Exchange Lines (DELs), with a waiting list of 28.87 lakh. The demand is projected to grow to 360-380 lakh DELs by the year 2001-2002. Thus 186-237 lakh additional DELs would have to be provided by the Government and the private sector during the Ninth Plan. In this, almost 52 lakh DELs are envisaged to be the private sector's contribution [4].

3. The cumulative investment up to the year 2001 to meet demand for cellular mobile and radio paging services is estimated at US$ 8 billion and US$ 1 billion respectively.

4. Investment in other Value Added Services (VAS) up to 2001 are estimated at US$ 3.5 billion.

5. The government cannot make investments of this magnitude because of resource limitations. The private sector and foreign companies are therefore welcomed into this sector, both as direct investors and exporters of equipment and technology.

6. Provision of Internet services has been thrown open to domestic and foreign investors with effect from October 7, 1998. A new policy for Internet Service Providers (ISPs) was announced in 1998 allowing independent service providers to enter the sector ending the earlier monopoly of VSNL.

7.2.4 Drawbacks: The following drawbacks of this sector are noteworthy.

1. VSAT (Very Small Aperture Terminal) services, though privatised, have not taken off in India. Demand for electronic mail, video-conferencing is not strong enough to justify investment. Besides, licence fees to be paid to the Department of Telecommunications are too high given the size of demand.

2. The DoT retains its monopoly as of now as the main service provider of short and long distance basic services. Private operators have to obtain licenses from DoT and work with it on a revenue sharing basis. It has been agreed in principle that private companies will be allowed to establish their own gateways in addition to using the gateways of DoT, VSNL or authorised public/government organisations. But this concept will be put into practice only after security-related issues are looked into by a committee that has already been set up.

3. Potential investors should be aware that telecom privatisation has been hit with snags. Cellular phone operators have been taken by unpleasant surprises. The average air-time use per subscriber per month is less than the estimates of both the bidders and the government. Each subscriber now spends an average of Rs.1,100 a month, but the industry needs a per subscriber expenditure of Rs. 1,800 every month to make commercial sense. This situation is

building pressure to extend the licenses to 15 year periods as opposed to the current 10 years. The extension will bring in extra revenue which can help the private operators make some money for themselves and pass a part of it to the customer as well (given the intense competition among the private operators).

4. One possibility is to charge a high monthly rental but low air-time charge. This may reduce the number of subscribers but those who subscribe will have a higher spending power. The profile of the cell-phone owner in India is therefore poised to change towards the better-off classes who can pay higher monthly rental and talk longer on cheaper air-time rates. This will drive out the lower middle classes from the cell-phone circuit, but middle-to-upper middle classes in India are huge enough to make commercial sense for the private operators.

7.3 Financial Services (Banking and Non-banking)

India has one of the most developed financial markets in the developing world. Tremendous scope exists for both banking and non-banking financial institutions from other countries. Top companies from the United Kingdom and the United States among others are already active in India's financial markets. Some of the foreign financial giants operating in India are: Merrill Lynch, Oppenheimer, J.P. Morgan, Morgan Stanley, Grindlays, Standard Chartered, Hong Kong and Shanghai Banking Corporation among others.

Banking Services: Foreign direct investment is permitted up to 20% and in the case of NRIs up to 40% in the banking sector. In case of short fall in foreign equity contribution by

NRIs , multilateral institutions are allowed to invest within the overall foreign equity of 40%.

Non-banking Financial Services: These include merchant banking, underwriting, portfolio management services, stock broking, asset management, venture capital funds, custodial services, factoring, leasing and finance, housing finance, credit and business etc.

The minimum capitalisation norms for these services are as follows:

- where FDI is less than 50%, US$ 0.5 million to be brought upfront.
- where FDI is greater than 50% but less than 75% , US$ 5 million to be brought upfront.
- where FDI is greater than 75% and less than or equal to 100%, US$ 50 million out of which US$ 7.5 million to be brought upfront and the balance in 24 months.

7.3.1 Prospects and Opportunities: 1. Considerable scope exists for providing modern and innovative service packages in the financial sector. The most promising sub-sectors of the financial services market are capital markets. venture banking, consumer financing, mutual funds, and infrastructure financing.

2. India already has foreign exchange reserves of US$ 27 billion which is considered very comfortable, but the country needs to use foreign skills and networks to be able to manage the huge sums for its development needs.

3. Local financial Institutions such as the Industrial Development Bank of India (IDBI), Industrial Credit and Investment Corporation of India (ICICI), Industrial Finance Corporation of India , Unit Trust of India and the Shipping Credit and Investment Corporation of India have raised

billions through the most sophisticated financial instruments including Deep Discount Bonds.

7.3.2 Insurance: After much dithering, India has finally opened up the insurance sector to private and foreign investors. Foreign investment and access to foreign capital by domestic companies has been progressively liberalised in India. The insurance sector, nationalised since 1971, has been opened up according to an announcement made in November 1998.

The financial year 1999-2000 witnessed a most significant reform with far reaching implications for long-term savings. This relates to the Insurance Regulatory and Development Authority (IRDA) Bill passed by the Parliament in December, 1999 which, inter alia;

1. gives statutory status to the interim Insurance Regulatory Authority,
2. opens up the insurance sector to the private providers,
3. allows foreign equity in domestic insurance companies subject to a maximum of 26% of the total paid-up capital, and
4. stipulates minimum paid-up capital of Rs.100 crore each for companies in life insurance and general insurance [5].

`The following facts show how under-developed the Indian insurance business is due to state monopoly and lack of aggressive marketing of insurance policies:

- Per capita insurance premium in India is a mere US$ 6, one of the lowest in the world. In South Korea, the corresponding figure is US$ 1,338.
- Insurance premium in India accounts for a mere 2 per cent of GDP(compared to the world average of 7.8 per cent).

- Insurance premium as a percentage of savings is barely 5.95 per cent in India (compared to 52.5 per cent in the UK).

The above figures show the huge scope that exists for new business in the insurance sector. Liberalisation will bring about strong marketing of policies by rival firms, which is expected to benefit the customer through a wider range of products and better services. Until now, policies have only been 'bought' by customers, rarely marketed by the insurance firms. Table 7.2 mentions, list of Indian companies entering the insurance sector and their foreign partners.

7.4 Food Processing

From a starving nation in 1947 when it won political independence, India today is one of the world's major producer of foodgrains. Though a major food producers, India accounts for less than 1.5 per cent of international food trade. This indicates vast scope for both investors and exporters. The industry requires massive investment over the coming years to create necessary infrastructure, expand production facilities and state-of-the-art- technology to match the international quality and standards.

The following points may be noted regarding the Government's policy towards foreign investment in this sector:

1. Foreign direct investment of around US$ 1 billion has already been approved in India's food processing industry since 1991.

2. Foreign investors can own 100 per cent equity in plants they set up. However, it is advisable to take a local partner. There has been some civilised resistance from ultra-

Table 7.2 List of Indian Companies Entering Insurance and Their Foreign Partners

Indian company	Foreign partner
Tata Group	AIG Insurance
Godrej	Rothschild (UK)
DCM Shriram Consolidated	Royal and Sun Alliance (UK)
HDFC	Standard Life (UK)
Bombay Burmah Trading	General Accident (Scotland, UK)
Kotak Mahindra	Chubb Insurance (US)
20th Century Finance	Canada Life Assurance (Canada)
Alpic Finance	Allianz Holding (Germany)
C.K. Birla Group	Zurich Insurance (Switzerland)
ICICI	Prudential (UK)
Hindustan Times	Commercial Union (UK)
Dabur	Liberty Mutual (UK)
Sanmar Group	GIO (Australia)
ITC	Eagle Star (UK)
Peerless	Guardian Royal Insurance (UK)
Sundaram Finance	Winterthur Ins (Switzerland)
M.A. Chidambaram Group	Metlife (UK)
Ranbaxy	Cigna (US)

nationalistic quarters of opinion to foreign food products. This resistance will be less if a local partner is involved.

7.4.1 Prospects and Opportunities: 1. Changing socio-economic conditions including breakdown of the joint-family system, increasing number of working women and Western influence (via TV channels) in the urban areas are fuelling a demand for packaged foods. The profile of the middle class is changing steadily and hired domestic help is becoming costlier. This is conducive to an expansion in demand for ready-to-eat Indian-style foods.

2. India already has all the requirements for a head-start in the food-processing industry. Basic materials such as foodgrains, pulses, vegetables and meats (non-beef) can be sourced locally or easily imported if local availability is inadequate.

3. India enjoys strong international competitiveness in fruit and vegetable based products as also marine products, thus providing high opportunities for exports of such items. In 1997-98, India exported processed fruits and vegetables worth US$ 173.5 million [6].

4. Many Indian firms are eagerly seeking foreign partners for joint-ventures to avail of their technological advantage.

5. Supermarkets are just beginning to appear in India's big cities and this is the time for international chains to set a foothold. Competition will only increase with time. International restaurant chains and foreign companies are being actively encouraged to enter the Indian food market for bringing in state-of-the-art processing and packaging along with new products; backward integration of technology , to improve raw material quality of farmers/livestock breeders; higher levels of sanitation and quality control; modern methods of mass marketing etc.

6. India's liberal intelligentsia is gradually building the opinion that foreign investments in the processed food sector will benefit rural agriculture, thus beating the nationalists with their own slogans. The liberal intelligentsia is gradually prevailing.

7.4.2 Promising Sub-sectors: The promising sub-sectors in the food processing industry for foreign direct investment include soft-drink bottling, confectionery manufacture, fishing, aquaculture, fish-processing, grain-milling and grain-based products, meat and poultry processing, alcoholic beverages, milk processing, tomato paste, snack food, fast-food, ready-to-eat breakfast cereals, ice-creams, refrigerated food handling, supermarkets, food additives, flavours etc.

The main sub-sectors along with the advantages offered by them are given below.

1. A potential processed food product is ***meat and poultry products***. India ranks first in world cattle population, and has 50 per cent of world buffalo population and one-sixth of world goat population. Buffalo meat is surplus in India. There is vast scope to set up modern slaughter facilities and cold store chains in meat and poultry processing sector. Compared with meat, poultry industry has registered significant growth. Both poultry and egg processing units have come in a very big way in the country. India is exporting egg powder, frozen egg yolk and albumin powder to Europe, Japan and other countries. Poultry exports are mostly to Maldives and Oman. Indian poultry meat products have good markets in Japan, Malaysia, Indonesia and Singapore.

2. ***Milk and milk products*** is rated as one of the most promising sectors which deserves foreign investment in a big way. The total milk production is around 72 million

tonnes and the demand for milk is estimated at around 80 million tonnes. Manufacture of casein and lactose, largely being imported presently, has good scope. Exports of milk products have been decanalised.

3. ***Grains*** could emerge as a major export earner for India in coming years. India's food grains production is now at around 225-230 million tones. These include rice, jawar, bajra, maize, wheat, gram and pulses. Indian basmati rice enjoys command in the international market. Besides growing Middle east market for basmati rice, many other countries are showing interest for this food grain. In 1997-98, export of basmati and non-basmati rice stood at US$ 907 million [7].

4. Among plantation, ***tea*** has emerged as major foreign exchange earner. India is the largest producer and exporter of black tea. India exported 210 million kilograms of tea in 1998 [8]. Of course, the scope of foreign investment in this sector is good and the multinational tea companies would either be trying for marketing joint ventures with the Indian producers or acquire stakes in Indian tea companies. There is strong possibilities of third country exports through such joint venture as quality wise still Indian teas are ruling the international market.

5. ***Alcoholic beverages*** is another area where India witnessed substantial foreign investment. Foreign investment in this sector is about 70 percent of the total investment made so far. The IMFL (Indian Made Foreign Liquor) primarily comprises wine, vodka, gin, whisky, rum and brandy. Draught beer is a comparatively recent introduction in the Indian market. One of the major advantages for any investor eyeing the Indian liquor market is that India offers enough raw materials like molasses,

barely, maize, potatoes, grapes, yeast and hops for the industry.

6. Yet another catchy investment sector is ***fisheries***. There is growing canned and processed fishes from India. The marine fish include prawns, shrimps, tuna, cuttlefish, squids, octopus, red snappers, ribbon fish, mackerel, lobsters, cat fish etc. In the past few years, there has been substantial foreign investment in fisheries. The potential could be gauged by the fact that against fish production potential in the Exclusive Economic Zone of 3.9 million tones, actual catch is to the tune of 2.87 million tones. Harvesting from inland sources is around 2.7 million tones. Fisheries sector has been recognised as a powerful income and employment generator, besides emerging as an important item in export trade. The value of export of marine products (including fish) during 1998-99 was Rs. 4,627 crore [9].

7.4.3 Drawbacks: The biggest bottleneck in expanding the food processing sector, in terms of both investment and exports, is lack of adequate infrastructure. Without a strong and dependable cold chain vital sector like food processing industry which is based mostly on perishable products cannot survive and grow. Even at current level of production, farm produce valued at Rs 70,000 million is being wasted every year only because there is no adequate storage, transportation, cold chain facilities and other infrastructure supports. Cold chain facilities are miserably inadequate to meet the increasing production of various perishable products like milk, fruits, vegetables, poultry, fisheries etc.

7.5 Transportation Industry

The transportation industry includes the automobile industry, air and sea transport, passenger cars, auto ancillaries or parts, ports etc.

7.5.1 Automobile Industry: India's automotive components industry is the most lucrative sector for foreign direct investments. Hundreds of collaborations foreign direct investments have been made in recent years and there is tremendous potential for more. Markets are huge and growing both within India and overseas. The Automotive Components Manufacturers Association (ACMA) represents this sector in India.

Prospects and Opportunities: 1. India offers a relatively low cost production base and is strategically positioned as a launching base for third country export to Asia-Pacific and European markets.

2. Growth in road transport, increasing urbanisation and privatisation of public transport will translate into growing demand for commercial vehicles.

3. The market is worth US$ 2.3 billion at present and this is expected to touch US$ 9.4 billion in 2001.

4. India has added advantage of an extensively segmented market and a well-developed dealer network.

5. Growth of consumer finance, leasing and hire-purchase options for vehicle dealers and buyers also boost demand.

6. A well developed components industry offers opportunities for sourcing. The scope is vast for foreign collaborations to produce branded models stressing on emission standards, fuel efficiency, advanced features and contemporary styles.

7. Automotive components manufactured in India are of top quality and used as original components for vehicles

made by such top international companies as General Motors, Mercedes, IVECO and Daewoo among others.

8. Japanese and British component manufacturers are already operating joint-ventures in India. American companies which have, or are planning to, set up plants in India include Delphi (an automotive components division of General Motors USA), Delco Electronics, Textron and Magna International of Canada.

7.5.2 Roads and Highways: Massive investments are envisaged in widening and/or strengthening existing highways, reconstructing/widening bridges, constructing expressways, upgradation initiatives especially in high density corridors. The following points are noteworthy regarding the policy of the Government.

1. The National Highway Act, 1956 was amended in June 1995 to provide for a legal framework for private sector participation in road development [10].

2. Private sector including foreign equity participation up to 100% in the highways is envisaged under Build Operate and Transfer (BOT) concept.

3. Automatic approval of foreign equity up to 74% for construction and maintenance of rail beds non-vehicular bridges, non-vehicular tunnels, rope ways and run ways and up to 100% for construction and maintenance of roads, highways, vehicular bridges, Govt. roads, vehicular tunnels, subject to foreign equity not exceeding Rs. 15 billion .

Prospects and Opportunities: 1. Investments worth an estimated US$ 34 billion is needed till 2005-06 for the development of National and State Highways. Out of this, the requirement of private sector investment is US$ 8.3 billion.

2. To encourage private sector participation, a Model Concession Agreement for major projects costing more than Rs. 100 crore has been finalised to be undertaken under BOT Scheme. Another Model Concession Agreement for projects less than Rs. 100 crore has also been finalised by Ministry of Surface Transport. To date, projects involving an investment of around Rs. 1000 crore have already been taken under the BOT scheme [11].

3. Projects relating to bypasses, bridges, and four laning of existing sections of National Highways, which on the basis of traffic density are financially viable and bankable, would be taken up through private sector participation [12].

4. Land acquisition, preliminary project preparation and operation of facilities will be undertaken by government free of cost and free of encumbrances.

5. Incentives include tax holidays, reduced custom duties on construction equipment etc.

7.5.3 Ports and Shipping: Government has initiated various steps to expand the infrastructural and management base of the key ports of the country. In order to encourage private sector including foreign equity participation in development of port facilities, policies and procedures have been significantly liberalised.

Following areas have been identified for private sector participation and investment:

1. Leasing out existing assets of the port,

2. Construction/creation of additional assets, such as:

(a)Construction and operation of container terminals.

(b) Construction and operation of bulk, break bulk, multipurpose and specialised cargo berths.

(c) Warehousing , container freight stations, storage facilities and tank farms.

(d) Cranage/handling equipment.
(e)Setting up of captive power plants.
(f) Dry docking and ship repair facilities.

3. Leasing of equipment for port handling and leasing of floating crafts from the private sector.
4. Pilotage.
5. Captive facilities for port based industries [13].

Foreign equity participation up to 100% is allowed for BOT PROJECTS. Automatic approval up to 74% foreign equity for construction and maintenance of ports and harbours has been allowed.

The shipping, ship building and ship repair sectors offer a number of incentives and opportunities to investors. Facilities at par with 100% Export Oriented Units (EOUs) are also available for the ship repair industry.

Prospects and Opportunities: 1. Significant potential exists for expansion of infrastructural and management base of key ports.

2. Considerable scope exists for construction, operation and maintenance of container terminals, cargo handling terminals, dry docking and ship repair facilities.

3. Opportunities also in areas of warehousing and storage, floating crafts, carnage services, dredging and general maintenance.

4. Options available for private participation include leave of assets and equipments; management contract for running port facilities or providing services; leasing of well-defined activities/services; transfer of ownership to private parties.

5. The Government has already awarded the project for construction, management, and maintenance of two berths

container terminal on BOT basis at Jawahar Lal Nehru Port (JNPT) to a consortium headed by an Australian firm.

7.5.4 Air Taxi Operation: The policy envisages encouraging private sector participation in air taxi operations. Foreign equity participation up to 40% and 100% NRI equity are allowed subject to the approval of FIPB. No direct or indirect equity participation by foreign airlines is allowed . However, foreign equity up to 74% has been allowed in the airport infrastructure under the automatic approval route.

Following are guidelines for air taxi operations:

1. Air taxi operators shall be air carriers engaged in air transportation of persons, their baggage and cargo.

2. Operations by the air taxi operators shall, except on routes not covered by any scheduled operator where an air taxi operator shall have the option to sell tickets . to individual passengers and where prior permission of DGCA for each flight will not be necessary, be charter and/or non-scheduled operations. It shall be necessary to obtain authorisation from the Director General of Civil Aviation (DGCA) for each individual flight and tickets will be sold to individual passengers.

3. Air taxi operations shall not be permitted to destinations outside India.

7.6 Mining and Metallurgy

The metallurgical and mineral industries constitute the bedrock of industrial sector as they provide the basic raw materials for most of the industries. India is well endowed with minerals of 84 types - 4 fuel based, 11 metallic, 49 non-metallic and 20 minor minerals. Due to the rich resource base, considerable scope exists for foreign and domestic private investment in mining and metallurgy for commercial exploitation of these resources.

The policy of the Government regarding private investment in this sector has the following salient features.

1. The Mines and Minerals (Regulation and Development) Act, 1957 was amended in January 1994 and a new Mineral Policy was announced. With this, the mining sector was thrown open to the private sector including foreign direct investment.

2. Foreign equity up to 50% in the mining sector would be automatic, except for gold, silver, and precious stones.

3. Foreign equity up to 74% in the mining services viz. shafting, reclamation of mines, surveys etc. would be automatic.

4. Foreign equity holding in excess of automatic holding will require prior approval of the FIPB. Foreign investment in the mining of gold, silver, diamond, and precious stones will also require approval of the FIPB.

7.6.1 Prospects and Opportunities: 1. Existence of high quality geological database makes exploration a low risk investment proposition.

2. Scope also exists for activities such as modernisation/ optimisation of operations, revamping/retrofitting of equipments, technology upgradation etc. that will help secure higher recoveries and extraction, facilitate value addition and sustain higher production levels.

3. India is endowed with huge reserves of bituminous coal of Paleozoic and Tertiary ages within the Coal-bed methane (CBM) window at depths of nearly 250-1200 metres. India wants foreign and domestic private companies for the exploration and commercial exploitation of CBM resources at some of the underground coal mines.

4. The mining lease period has been increased to a maximum of 30 years and a minimum of 20 years to provide greater stability of tenure to leaseholders. The prospecting period has also been increased from 2 to 3 years and further renewal up to a period not exceeding 5 years is allowed to facilitate more systematic and scientific prospecting and exploration for mineral deposits.

7.7 Hotels and Tourism

Economic liberalisation has given a new impetus to the hospitality industry. Many foreign companies have already tied up with prominent Indian companies for setting up new hotels, motels and holiday resorts. The entry of McDonald's, Pepsico's Kentucky Fried Chicken, Domino's and Pizza Hut have given an international glitz to the hospitality sector.

The term *hotels* includes, *inter alia*, restaurants, beach resorts and other tourist complexes providing accommodation and /or catering and food facilities to tourists. The term *tourism related industry* includes, *inter alia*, the following:

1. Travel agencies, tour operating agencies and tourist transport operating agencies.
2. Units providing facilities for cultural or wildlife experience and adventure to tourists.
3. Surface, air and water transport facilities for tourists.
4. Leisure, entertainment, amusement, sports and health unit for tourists.
5. Convention/seminar units and organisations.

Over the years, tourism has emerged as a major segment of the Indian economy contributing substantially to the foreign exchange earnings which have increased from Rs.4,892 crore in 1991-92 to Rs. 10,417 crore in 1996-97.

Foreign investment up to 51% equity for establishing Hotels and Tourism Related Industries can be made through automatic route. Foreign investment above 51% equity will require approval of Govt. (FIPB).

7.7.1 Prospects and Opportunities: 1. The Indian hospitality industry is growing at a rate of 15 percent annually. The current gap between supply and demand is expected to widen further as the economy opens and grows. The government forecasts an additional requirement of 200,000 rooms by the turn of the century.

2. Several international chains including Sheraton, Holiday Inn, Intercontinental, Hyatt, Radisson, BestWestern, Days Inn, Hilton, Quality Inn, Ramada Inn, Meridien, Kempenski, Four Seasons Regent, Accor, and Marriott International are entering or expanding their hotel network in India.

3. A rapidly growing middle class, the advent of corporate incentive travel and the multinational companies into India has boosted prospects for tourism. India's easy visa rules, public freedoms and its many attractions as an ancient civilisation makes tourism development easier than in many other countries.

4. There is scope for development of tourism related services like travel and tour operating agencies, transportation and other services providing leisure, entertainment, sports and health units, convention facilities etc.

5. Incentives include interest and capital subsidies, tax exemption, special foreign exchange facilities, concessional duties on imports of capital equipment etc.

6. There is availability of trained manpower for the development of a service sector like hotels and tourism. At

present, there are 20 Institutes of Hotel Management and Catering Technology and 13 Foodcraft Institutions functioning in the country. A number of institutes have also started coming up in private sector since it can find adequate number of trainees with the required paying capacity.

7.8 Electronics

The electronics industry constitute 7.28% of the total approved investment in the post-liberalisation period. It includes electrical equipment, computer software industry, electronics, computer hardware etc. The present low level of penetration provides tremendous potential for immediate market expansion in almost every segment of electronics.

7.8.1 Prospects and Opportunities: 1. Consumer electronics is a high growth sector which also has an active replacement market.

2. Control and industrial electronics face increasing demand from projects in power, refineries, petrochemicals, cement etc. Demand for test and measuring instruments will be growing with the rapid development of communications.

3. A strong base exists for the manufacture of micro-computers, mini-computers and mainframe computer system; work stations and other manufactured products like floppy disk drivers, printers, CRT terminals, keyboards and plotters.

4. In the software area, India has the third largest pool of software writing talent with world-class skills and at relatively low cost, thus, providing tremendous outsourcing opportunities.

5. The electronic component sector provides opportunities for joint ventures and contract manufacturing

activities in areas like semi-conductors, ICs, chip capacitors, PCBs etc.

6. The policy provides foreign equity participation up to 100% and several incentives/concessions for EOUs, EHTPs and STPs.

7. A high powered National Task Force on IT and Software Development was set up by the Prime Minister's Office on May 22, 1998, under the Chairmanship of the Deputy Chairman of Planning Commission. The first report of the taskforce on IT Action Plan has brought about a new paradigm in setting up IT software and hardware manufacturing units for making them viable for meeting the local demands as well as exports by creating a policy ambience and investment climate in the country comparable to those in Taiwan, Malaysia, and Singapore.

7.9 Conclusion

The initial policy stimulus to foreign direct investment in India came in July 1991 when the new industrial policy provided, *inter alia*, automatic approval for projects with foreign equity participation up to 51 per cent in high priority areas. In recent years, the Government has initiated the second generation reforms under which measures have been taken to further facilitate and broaden the base of foreign direct investment in India. The policy for FDI allows freedom of location, choice of technology, repatriation of capital and dividends. As a result of these measures, there has been a strong surge of international interest in the Indian economy. The rate at which foreign direct investment inflow has grown during the post- liberalisation period is a clear indication that India is fast emerging as an attractive destination for overseas investors.

In spite of the fact that India is a strategic location with access to a vast domestic and South Asian market, its share in world's total flow of direct investment to developing countries is a meagre 1.5 per cent. This calls for further liberalisation of norms for investment by present and prospective foreign entrepreneurs. Attracting foreign capital requires an investor-friendly environment. It underlines the need for efficient and adequate infrastructural facilities, availability of skilled and semi-skilled labour force, business-friendly public administration and moderate rates of taxation.

A disquieting trend has been noticed in recent years that a sizeable amount of FDI is used for acquiring Indian companies rather than creating new productive assets. This has involved only a change of ownership of the existing assets without adding to the productive capacity of the economy. This tendency needs to be discouraged. FDI becomes meaningful only when new capacities are created in the economy or the existing capacities are made more efficient and competitive.

As per Economic Survey, 2000-2001, engineering industry attracted the largest volume of FDI inflows with the sector aggregating FDIs worth US $ 326 million. Electronics and electrical equipment industries were the second largest recipient of FDI inflows. Pharmaceutical industry witnessed almost a 100 per cent jump in FDI inflows in 1999-2000 standing at US $ 54 million as compared to US $ 28 million in 1998-99.

With a huge demand-supply gap still existing in the infrastructure sector, there seems ample scope for more foreign investments in this region. A more simplistic, investor-friendly and committed policies by the Government will definitely attract the attention of world economy. With our population burgeoning to 102 crore as on 1.3.2001 as per latest census of 2001, the need for basic facilities is bound to increase. Definitely foreign investment is required to fill this huge gap as the Indian economy is already reeling under resource crunch.

Notes

1. Government of India, Ministry of Finance, *Economic Survey*, 1999-2000, p. 153.

2. *Ibid.*, p. 153.

3. Government of India, Planning Commission, *Ninth Five Year Plan* (1997-2002), Volume II, p. 869.

4. *Ibid.*, pp. 872-73.

5. *Economic Survey*, 1999-2000, *op cit.*, p. 60.

6. Reserve Bank of India, *Handbook of Statistics on Indian Economy*, 1999, p. 162.

7. *Ibid.*, p.162.

8. *Economic Survey*, 1999-2000, *op cit.*, p. 135.

9. *Economic Survey*, 1999-2000, *op cit.*, p. 138.

10. *Ninth Five Year Plan* (1997-2002), *op cit.*, Volume II, p. 801.

11. *Economic Survey*, 1999-2000, *op cit.*, p. 157.

12. *Ninth Five Year Plan* (1997-2002), *op cit.*, Volume II, p. 801.

13. *Ninth Five Year Plan* (1997-2002), *op cit.*, Volume II, pp. 816-17.

Chapter 8

Foreign Investment in India: Prospects and Opportunities

8.1 Foreign Investors and the Indian Market

Foreign investment in India has grown substantially in the last decade following the liberalisation of Indian economy in 1991. Certain booming sectors of our economy, specially the infrastructure has attracted considerable attention. We study hereby the future outlook of investment potential in various sectors of Indian economy.

8.1.1 Is India an Attractive FDI Destination ?

The extent and spread of international production activity may be gauged from the number of enterprises that are involved in it and their location. Over 500,000 foreign affiliates are in operation world-wide, established by about 60,000 parent companies spanning virtually every country in the world.

The establishment of foreign affiliates involves costs - in cash or kind, tangible and intangible. Some of the funds required are made available by parent firms in the form of equity (often in a package comprising capital as well as other resources such as technology, organisational and managerial practices and marketing expertise), intra-company loans, and reinvested earning together defined as foreign direct investment (FDI). In addition, foreign affiliates can also be financed from funds that they raise in the domestic capital markets of host countries or in international capital markets in forms such as loans and bonds. Flows of funds from international capital markets may in fact sometimes be higher than FDI flows.

MNCs operating from Indian soil have given India 'an attractive FDI destination billing' and are planning to expand their operations in the country. A recent FICCI study, submitted to the Finance Minister, highlighted the fact that despite the hue and cry about lack of infrastructure and market penetration, MNC's in the country are quite pleased with India's growth conditions, when compared with markets in the West.

Meanwhile, the cumulative FDI approval by the government between January 1991 and September 2000, stood at $ 27 billion and total inflows amounted to $ 22.4 billion.

In the first half of the year 2000, FDI flows from NRI direct investment and acquisition of shares of Indian companies by non-resident Indians (NRIs) were lower in relation to the previous year. India attracted the highest amount of FDI in 1997-98 when the country received an inflow of $ 3.55 billion.

In the total FDI flows, the engineering industry has been at the top of the list with its share being $ 326 million in 1999-2000. The other major sectors in which relatively higher FDI flows were channelised were electronics and electrical equipment, followed by pharmaceuticals. Food and dairy industries registered a sharp increase in FDI flows - up from $ 19 million in 1998-99 to $ 121 million in 1999-2000. In pharma also, FDI flows almost doubled from $ 28 million to $ 54 million.

8.1.2 Flow of Funds: Origin

Among the investors, Mauritius and the US continued to be the largest sources of FDI for India although inflows from Mauritius were lower during the year at $ 501 million compared to $ 590 million in 1998-99. In the case of the US also, the situation was similar with inflows dropping from $ 543 in 1998-99 to $ 355 million in 1999-2000.

Mauritius has emerged as the largest source of foreign direct investment (FDI) into India during January-September 2000. Statistics put together by the Confederation of Indian Industry (CII) show that FDI worth $ 1.10 billion from the Island nation was approved during the period. This is 25 per cent more than its nearest rival, the US, from which FDI of $ 877 million was approved during the nine-month period.

In fact, Mauritius is the only country from which FDI of over a billion dollars was approved during January-September 2000. The approvals include that from the Foreign Investment Promotion Board, the Secretariat of Industrial Approvals and the Reserve Bank of India.

On a cumulative basis, the US continues to be the largest source of FDI into India - between January 1991 and September 2000. FDI of $ 14.12 billion from the country was approved. Mauritius comes next with FDI approvals of $ 7.05 billion. Interestingly, FDI approvals from Mauritius stood at zero for 1991, the first year of economic reforms, as well as 1992. It started trickling in 1993 with approvals of $ 40.74 million in 1993 and crossed the billion mark in 1997 when it touched $ 2.87 billion.

A total of 170 collaborations were approved from Mauritius during January-September 2000. While 168 of these were financial collaborations, only two were technical collaborations. This, however, was far short of the 397 collaborations okayed from the US during the same period, out of which, 323 were financial collaborations and 74 were technical collaborations.

Between January 1991 and September 2000, 741 collaborations from Mauritius received the nod' while 711 of these were financial collaborations, and 30 were technical collaborations. The reason for Mauritius emerging as a favoured source of FDI into the country is the lower income tax rates prevailing here. Like most other countries, it has a double taxation avoidance agreement with Mauritius.

It means that any foreign investor has the option of paying tax either in India or in Mauritius. Since the tax rates prevailing in that country are amongst the highest in the world, many multinational corporations prefer to have their investments through Mauritius.

8.2 Foreign Direct Investment: Government's Policy

A wider liberalisation of the foreign direct investment (FDI) regime is under way, given the declining trend in inflows and the fall in India's share among developing countries in 1999, going by the pointers in this year's Economic Survey. With FDI inflows of $ 2.15 billion in 1999-2000 being lower compared to the previous year ($ 2.46 billion), and the share in global FDI flows among the developing countries sliding from two per cent in 1997 to one per cent in 1999, there is a cause for concern. This also underlines the need for even greater policy reforms in the FDI regime.

The Government has identified 17 areas where higher FDI limits will be permitted. These include drugs and pharmaceuticals, telecommunications, civil aviation, tourism and the hospitality industry, non-banking finance companies (NBFCs) and defence production to name a few.

According to the Economic Survey, 2000-2001, although FDI flows have slipped during 1999-2000, the bright spot has been that inflows during the current year i.e. 2000-2001, are showing signs of improvement. During April to September 2000, aggregate FDI inflows have been higher at $ 1.91 billion compared to $ 1.48 billion during the corresponding period last year.

As part of the economic reforms programme, policy and procedures governing foreign investment and technology transfer have been significantly simplified and streamlined. Today, foreign investment is freely allowed in all sectors including the services sector except a few sensitive sectors like defence, atomic energy, real estate etc.

8.2.1 Trade Policy - Year 2001

- Targeted export growth rate of 18 per cent to reach 1 per cent of total world exports of US $ 7.5 trillion by the year 2004.
- Promotion of international trade on agricultural goods with a 'farm-to-poor' approach in the Agri-Economic Zones.
- Market Access Initiative: Government would assist the industry in research and development, market research, specific market and product studies, warehousing and retail marketing infrastructure in select countries and direct market promotion activity through media advertising and buyer-seller meets.
- Setting up of Business-cum-Trade Facilitation Centre and Trade portal in Pragati Maidan, New Delhi.
- Strengthening of the annual Advance Licensing Scheme.

- Special Economic Zones (SEZs): In addition to the facilities announced in the Trade Policy 2000, SEZ developers to be given infrastructure status under the Income Tax Act and concessional duty for procurement of goods for setting up SEZs.
- Quantitative Restrictions were removed for 714 items in the Trade Policy 2000. Quantitative Restrictions for the remaining 715 items to be removed in the current Trade Policy.
- Safeguard measures to ensure safety and security of the citizens and bio-security concerns initiated.

8.2.2 FDI Approvals: Policies and Procedures

All items/activities except the following are under the automatic route for foreign direct investment (FDI):

1. All proposals that require an industrial licence. An industrial licence is mandatory if:

(a) the item involved requires an industrial licence under the Industries (Development and Regulation) Act 1951 or

(b) the foreign equity portion is more than 24 per cent of the equity capital of units manufacturing items reserved for small scale industries; or

(c) the item concerned requires an industrial licence in terms of the locational policy.

2. All proposals in which the foreign collaborator has a previous venture or tie-up in India (excluding IT Sector).

3. All proposals relating to the acquisition of shares in an existing Indian company in favour of a foreign investor.

4. All proposals outside the notified sectoral policy caps, or under sectors in which FDI is not permitted.

Investment in Export Oriented Units (EOUs) and units in Export Processing Zones (EPZs), Special Economic Zones

(SEZs), Software Technology Parks (STPs) and Electronics Hardware Technology parks (EHTPs) also qualify for the automatic route, subject to notified sectoral policy and equity caps.

FDI in the insurance sector upto 26 per cent is allowed under the automatic route subject to licence from the Insurance Regulatory and Development Authority for undertaking insurance activities.

In addition to automatic approval for new companies, such approvals can also be granted for existing companies proposing to induct foreign equity. For existing companies with an expansion programme, the additional requirements are that:

i) the increase in equity level must result from the expansion of the equity base of the existing company;

ii) the money to be remitted should be in foreign currency; and

iii)the proposed expansion programme should be predominantly in the sector(s) under automatic route.

For existing companies, without an expansion programme, the additional requirements for eligibility for automatic approval are:

i) they should be engaged predominantly in industries under the automatic route;

ii) the increase in equity level must be from expansion of the equity base; and

iii)the foreign equity must come in foreign currency.

Otherwise, the proposal would need Government approval through the Foreign investment Promotion Board (FIPB), which is required to take a decision within 30 days.

Investors coming through the Automatic Route are required to file relevant documents with the Reserve Bank of

India within 30 days after the issue of shares to foreign investors. Proposals which do not fulfil the conditions for automatic approval will require the approval of the Government. The investors have to make an application to the Foreign investment Promotion Board, Ministry of Commerce and Industry, Udyog Bhawan, New Delhi for obtaining such approval.

The reform process has deregulated the economy and stimulated domestic and foreign investments, taking India firmly into the forefront of investment destinations. The Government, keen to promote investment in the country has radically simplified and rationalised policies, procedures and regulatory aspects. Foreign investment is welcome in almost all sectors, except those of strategic concern (for instance, defence and atomic energy).

8.2.3 Incentives for Investments

A series of incentives has been announced to promote investments. These include import of capital goods of concessional customs duty (subject to fulfilment of certain export obligations), liberalisation of external commercial borrowing norms, tax holiday, and concessional tax treatment for certain sectors. In addition, several State Governments offer incentives, such as subsidy on fixed capital, loans of concessional rates of interest, and attractive power rates. While several incentives are project specific, a number of firms have been successful in negotiating favourable investment terms with the State Governments concerned.

Since the initiation of the economic liberalisation process in 1991, sectors such as automobiles, chemicals, food processing, oil and natural gas, petrochemicals, power, services and telecommunications have attracted considerable investments. Today, in the changed investment climate, India offers exciting business opportunities in virtually every sector of the economy.

8.3 FDI in India - Where the Opportunity Lies ?

We now discuss in detail the most sought after sectors of Indian economy where huge potential for foreign investment lies. The Indian governments' investment policy to invite huge investments as also the special promotion drives are discussed hereby.

A. The Power Sector

The 1991 Power Policy seeks to attract significant private sector investment in the Indian power sector. The key initiatives include:

- Private sector permitted to set up coal, gas or liquid based thermal projects, hydel projects and wind or solar projects of any size;
- Foreign equity participation brought under automatic approval for generation, transmission and distribution of power generated in hydro-electric, oil gas based and coal/lignite based power projects.
- Role of the Central Government curtailed and the State Governments and State Electricity Boards (SEBs) empowered to negotiate directly with developers, facilitating speedy clearances for the investor.
- Ancillary sector such as coal significantly deregulated.
- 100 per cent foreign equity permitted.

Potential

Demand is expected to grow to 570 billion Kwh by 2001-02 and to 782 Kwh by 2006-07. Over the 10 year period from 1997-2007, a total capacity addition of 98,000 MW is envisaged, entailing an investment of Rs. 5,750 billion in power generation, transmission and distribution.

The specific project opportunities expected in the near future include:

Liquid Fuel Based Projects using low sulphur heavy stock (LSHS), furnace oil (FO), heavy petroleum stock (HPS), Naphtha, Vacuum Residue, Condensate and Orimulsion are permitted by the Government. Import of liquefied natural gas (LNG) is also being considered for setting uplarge capacity combined cycle power plants. Transmission projects for power transfer are available for competitive bidding by the Central Transmission Utility (Power Grid) and State Transmission Utilities (SEBs/Grid Corporations). The transmission system projects are being identified for competitive bidding by the Central and State Transmission Utilities.

Attractive investment opportunities are likely to develop in distribution of power as several state governments have agreed to allow the gradual entry of the private sector in distribution.

B. Non-Conventional Energy Sources

Foreign Investors can enter into a joint venture with an Indian partner for financial and/or technical collaboration and also for setting up of renewable energy based power generation projects. The liberalised foreign investment approval regime is aimed at facilitating foreign investment and transfer of technology through joint ventures. 100 per cent foreign investment as equity is permissible. Government of India is encouraging foreign investors to set up renewable energy based power generation projects on Build-Own-Operate basis.

Potential

In India, investment opportunities are available for the following types of investors and users:

- Investment by foreign investors for manufacturing of renewable energy systems and devices based on:
  Wind, Solar Photo-voltaic, Solar Thermal, Small Hydro, Biomass, Co-generation, Geothermal, Tidal and Urban and Industrial Wastes for their utilisation in India and also for exports to developing and Third World countries.

C. Oil and Natural Gas

The Government has announced significant new policy initiatives to attract foreign investment in exploration and production.

Oil and gas fields are open to the private sector as well as for foreign participation under production sharing contracts. Foreign investment is to be permitted up to:

- 100 per cent in small sized oil fields;
- 60 per cent for unincorporated joint ventures and 51 per cent for incorporated joint ventures;
- 100 per cent for exploration and production of blocks identified under the New Exploration Licensing Policy.

The level of FDI in the refining sector under automatic approval has been raised from 49 per cent to 100 per cent. For 100 per cent EOU refineries, 100 per cent FDI is permitted.

For gas fields developed in the private sector, promoters are free to market the gas at market related prices.

For the petroleum products and pipeline sector, FDI is permitted upto 51 per cent.

FDI is permitted upto 74 per cent in infrastructure related to manufacturing and marketing of petroleum products.

100 per cent wholly owned subsidiary (WOS) is permitted for purpose of market study and formulation.

100 per cent wholly owned subsidiary is permitted for investment/financing.

For actual trading and marketing, minimum 26 per cent Indian equity is required over 5 years.

Potential

Total sedimentary basins, including deep waters 3.14 million sq. kms (41 per cent of this is still unexplored).

The present domestic gas supply is only 65 MMSCMD. The increasing demand-supply gap is expected to be met by imports.

Large demand for natural gas:

Year	Demand (MMSCMD)
1999	110
2002	151
2007	231
2012	313
2025	391

MMSCMD: Million Standard Cubic Meters per day

Development of Infrastructure

	1998-99	2024-25
Product Pipeline		
Capacity (MMTpa)	28.85	166
Part Capacity (MMT)	111.00	361

D. The Coal Sector

Private Indian companies setting up or operating power projects as well as coal or lignite mines for captive consumption are allowed FDI up to 100 per cent.

100 per cent FDI is allowed for setting up coal processing plants subject to the condition that the company shall not do coal mining and shall not sell washed coal or sized coal from its coal processing plants in the open market and shall supply the washed or sized coal to those parties who are supplying raw coal to coal processing plants for washing or sizing.

FDI up to 74 per cent is allowed for exploration or mining of coal or lignite for captive consumption. In all the above cases, FDI is allowed up to 50 per cent under the Automatic Route subject to the condition that such investment shall not exceed 49 per cent of the equity of a PSU.

E. Telecommunication

In Basic, Cellular, Mobile, Paging and Value Added Service, and Global mobile personnel communications by satellite, FDI is limited to 49 per cent subject to grant of licence from the Department of Telecommunications and adherence by the companies (who are investing and the companies in which investment is being made) to the licence conditions for foreign equity cap and lock-in period for transfer and addition of equity and other licence provisions.

FDI upto 100 per cent is allowed for the following activities in the telecom sector.

a. ISPs not providing gateways (both for satellite and submarine cables);

b. Infrastructure Providers providing dark fibre (IP category I);

c. Electronic Mail; and

d. Voice Mail.

Upto 100 per cent FDI in telecom manufacturing activities on automatic approval basis.

Potential

There exists an enormous demand-supply gap for basic services, with the average waiting period for telephone connections exceeding one year. Table 8.1 depicts the potential existing in the telecom sector.

Internet Services

There is no restriction on the number of Internet Service Providers (ISPs). No licence fee is payable up to October 31, 2003; thereafter a token licence fee of Re. 1 per annum is payable. ISPs are free to fix their own tariff; ISPs have been permitted to establish their own international gateways for carrying Internet traffic. They can obtain transmission link on lease from DTS, licensed basic service providers, railways, SEBs, Power Grid Corporation or any other operator specially authorised to lease such lines. ISPs can also establish their own transmission link within their service area if such links are not available from any of the authorised agencies.

Basic Telephone Services

Basic service providers are permitted to establish last mile linkages and carry their own long distance traffic within their service area. They are to be permitted direct inter-connectivity and sharing of infrastructure with other

Table 8.1: Demand-Supply Status of Various Services in India's Telecom Sector

Sector	Current Size	Projections
Basic Service	19 million lines	Additional 64 million lines required over the next 9 years to meet the demand for basic services; 20.4 million lines expected to be provided by the private sector.
Cellular Services	0.9 million subscribers	Cellular subscribers expected to cross 1.6 million by March 2000*.
Radio Paging	0.8 million subscribers	1.5 million subscribers expected by the end of financial year 2000.
Very Small Aperture Terminal (VSAT)	6,000	VSAT demand estimated at 11,000 shared hubs and dedicated hub terminals by 2000.
Internet	150,000	2 million Internet subscribers expected by the year 2000.

* The number of cellular subscribers has reached 3.27 million by January 2001.

basic service providers or any other type of service providers in their area of operation.

Cellular Mobile Services

Cellular service providers are permitted to carry their own long distance traffic within their service area. They are to be permitted direct inter-connectivity and sharing of infrastructure with other cellular service providers or any other type of service providers in their area of operation.

National Long Distance Services

As per the National Telecom Policy, '99, National Long Distance Services (NLD) beyond the service area shall be opened for competition. With a view to providing choice to consumers and promoting competition, all access providers would be mandatarily required to provide interconnection to all NLD providers.

Global Mobile Personal Communication by Satellite (GMPCS)

There is no restriction on the number of GMPCS licences and licences are issued on first-come-first-served basis. Gateways for GMPCS are to be located in India and operation and maintenance of the same are to be with an organisation designated by the Government. A two-tier licence fee is payable - a fixed component plus a variable component as percentage of revenues.

Other Value Added Services

As the telecommunications and Information Technology (IT) infrastructure in the country is expanding, there is a surge in demand for a range of value added services. The scheme for value added services has been considerably liberalised. These services include radio paging, public mobile radio trunking and domestic data using VSATs. Evolving of new services - Tele-education, Tele-medicine,

Tele-banking, Call Centre - is catching up with the Indian industry and has recently witnessed significant investments from domestic and foreign investors.

F. Information Technology

Automatic approval for foreign equity in software and almost all areas of electronics. Automatic approval accorded for foreign technology agreements in all areas of electronics except aerospace and defence, subject to specified conditions.

100 per cent foreign investment permitted in units set up exclusively for exports. Such units can be set up under any one of the schemes e.g. EHTPs, STPs, Free Trade Zones/EPZs, and 100 per cent EOUs.

Potential

According to a recent World Bank study, India is the preferred location for software vendors for its quality and cost. India has strong Unix base which provides opportunity for the development of products for internal based applications. Further, India has global connectivity with international dialing facility from over 13,220 locations. Leased/Switched high-speed data links from major centres through STPs and VSNL for point-to-point communication are also available. Internet connectivity is provided through several networks. Abundant investment opportunities exist in the following thrust areas in India:

(i) Communication infrastructure;
(ii) Optic Fibre Cable;
(iii) Gateways;
(iv) Satellite based Communication;
(v) Wireless;
(vi) Software Development;
(vii) IT-enabled Services;

(viii) IT Education (100,000 post-graduate professionals in IT required annually by 2004);

(ix) IT-enabled Education;

(x) Data Centres and Server Farms.

G. E-Commerce

Upto 100 per cent is permitted for B2B e-commerce, subject to the condition that the companies connected would divest 26 per cent of their equity in favour of the Indian public in five years, if the companies are listed in other parts of the world.

Potential

According to a study by ICRA Ltd., the volume of e-business in India is likely to increase from the level of Rs. 4.7 billion in 1999-2000 to a level above Rs. 250 billion in the next three to four years. The figure makes a clear case for large scale investments in the Indian e-commerce sector.

Direct to Home (DTH) Broadcasting Services

DTH TV services in Ku Band is now permitted; total foreign equity including FDI/NRI/OCB/FII is limited to 49 per cent. Within this limit FDI controlled by foreign investors through FDI/NRI/OCB investments should not exceed 20%. Broadcasting and/or cable network companies are not eligible to collectively own more than 20% of the total equity of the applicant company. Indian management control is a must.

H. Pharmaceuticals

Automatic approval for up to 74% foreign equity in the case of bulk drugs, their intermediates and formulations (except those produced by the use of recombinant DNA technology).

Potential

Indian pharmaceutical industry has shown tremendous progress in terms of infrastructure development, technology base and range of production. India derives its technological strengths in pharmaceuticals on the following bases:

- Self reliance displayed by the production of 70% of bulk drugs and almost the entire requirement of formulations within the country.
- Low cost of production.
- Low R&D costs.
- Innovative scientific manpower.
- Strength of National Laboratories.
- Increasing balance of trade in Pharma sector.

I. Chemicals

The chemical industry in India is well established and has recorded a steady growth in the overall Indian industrial scenario. The chemical and allied industries have been amongst the faster growing segments of the Indian industry. The Indian chemical industry had a turnover of around Rs. 900 billion in 1996-97. The chemical industry also accounted for over 10% of total Indian exports during 1997-98. The chemical industry is highly heterogeneous encompassing many sectors like organic and inorganic chemicals, dyestuffs, paints and pesticides. Some of the prominent individual chemical industries are caustic soda, soda ash, carbon black, phenol, acetic acid, methanol and azo dyes.

Potential

Currently, there is tremendous scope for growth in the chemical sector. The per capita consumption of chemicals in India is well below the prevailing world level. For instance, in sulphuric acid, which is considered the barometer of growth in the chemical industry, the per capita consumption is only about 5 kg per annum in India as compared to 40 kg in industrially developed countries.

J. Biotechnology

The setting up of a separate Department of Biotechnology (DBT) under the Ministry of Science and Technology in 1986 gave a new impetus to the development of modern biology and biotechnology in India. In more than a decade of its existence, the department has promoted and accelerated the pace of development of biotechnology in the country.

In India, concerted efforts for over a decade in R & D in the identified areas of modern biology and biotechnology have paid rich dividends. The proven technologies at the laboratory level have been scaled up and demonstrated in field. Patenting of innovations, technology transfer to industries and close interaction with them have given a new direction to biotechnology research.

Necessary guidelines for transgenic plants, recombinant vaccines and drugs have also been evolved. A strong base of indigenous capabilities has been created.

Potential

Biotechnology industry is seen as a research arm to Agritech, and Pharma industry with increased potential for strategic alliances. Global trends show that all large pharmaceutical players are putting their money in health care for long term benefits. It is expected that nearly half the drugs in the next decade would be biotech products.

Tremendous potential exists in agri business in an agrarian economy like India. There is a tremendous potential for transgenic seeds, bio-fertilisers etc. Number of small firms is high and also it is a knowledge based research intensive industry, with low capital requirements. This is depicted in Table 8.2.

Table 8.2: Biotechnology Sector: Status and Scope

(in million US $)

Sector	Turnover (1997)	Estimated turnover for 2000	Estimated turnover for 2005
Health Care Products	650	800	1,300
Agriculture	480	650	1,100
Industrial Products	556	647	830
Total (including others)	1,790	2,100	3,240

The field of biotechnology both for new innovations and applications would form a major research and commercial endeavour to socio-economic development in this decade.

K. Roads

FDI up to 100% under automatic route is permitted in projects for construction and maintenance of roads, highways, vehicular bridges, toll roads, vehicular tunnels, ports and harbours.

Potential

Investments worth an estimated US $ 34 billion needed till 2005-06 for the development of National and State Highways. Of this figure, the requirement of private sector investment is US $ 8.3 billion.

Opportunities exists in:

- highway construction
- four-laning of over 35,000 km of National Highways.

- highway related enroute activities like restaurants, motels, and rest/parking areas as may be decided by the implementing agency.

Select Project opportunities include:
Chennai-Nellore (US $ 350 million)
Bangalore-Chennai (US $ 305 million)
Surat-Manar (US $ 180 million)
Jaipur-Ajmer (US $ 147 million)

L. Ports

The principal legislations governing Indian ports are the Indian Ports Act, 1908, and The Major Ports Trust Act, 1963. The Indian Government recently announced a series of measures to promote foreign investment in the port sector, as listed below:

- No approval required for foreign equity up to 51% in projects providing supporting services to water transport, such as operation and maintenance of piers, loading and discharging of vehicles.

- Automatic approval for foreign equity up to 100% in construction and maintenance of ports and harbours. however, if the total foreign equity investment exceeds Rs. 15 billion, the proposal will be referred to the FIPB.

Open tenders are to be invited for private sector participation on a Build-Operate-Transfer (BOT) basis. Evaluation of bids will be based on the maximum realisation to the ports on a net present value basis. The maximum licence period will not exceed 30 years and at the end of the BOT period all assets will revert to the port in accordance with the conditions of the agreement.

The Government has announced guidelines for private/foreign participation that permit formation of joint ventures between major ports and foreign ports, between major ports and minor ports, and between major ports and companies.

The measures are aimed at attracting new technology, fostering strategic alliances with minor ports to create an optimal port infrastructure and enhancing private sector confidence in the funding of ports.

Potential

The areas identified for privatisation or investment by the private sector include:

(i) Leasing out of existing port assets
(ii) Creation of additional assets;
(iii) Construction or operation of container terminals;
(iv) Construction or operation of bulk, breck-bulk,
(v) Multipurpose and specialised cargo berths;
(vi) Warehousing,
(vii) Container freight stations,
(viii) Storage
(ix) Facilities and tank farms cranage and handling
(x) Equipment setting up captive power plants;
(xi) Dry docking and ship repair facilities.
(xii) Leasing of equipment and floating craft from the private sector.
(xiii) Pilotages
(xiv) Captive facilities for port based industries.

The guidelines permit the formation of a joint venture between a major port and foreign ports for the purposes of constructing new port facilities within existing ports, improving productivity of existing ports, and development of new port; Joint venture between major port trust and a minor port for improvements in the existing minor ports, the co-ordinated development of ports or in case of a situation where there are constraints in the economic expansion of the major ports; and a major port trust and a company or a consortium of companies where:

- a company or a consortium of companies, selected through a BOT bidding under the guidelines of private sector participation, alliances with a major port trust for improving the viability of the scheme and/or to enhance the confidence of the private sector.

- a company or a consortium of companies is selected under the scheme of innovative/unsolicited proposals.

- oil PSUs/a joint venture company of oil PSUs are/is selected for oil related port facility as a port based industry.

M. Civil Aviation

The monopoly of public sector air carriers ended with the repealing of the Air Corporation Act, 1953 on March 1, 1994.

- Automatic approval for foreign equity participation in airport infrastructure is allowed upto 100 per cent.

- Foreign equity upto 40 per cent; Investment by Non-Resident Indians upto 100 per cent permitted in domestic air transport services.

- Equity from foreign airlines not allowed in domestic air-transport services either directly or indirectly.

- Foreign Financial institutions allowed to hold equity in the domestic air-transport sector provided they do not have foreign airlines as their shareholders.

- Foreign investors allowed to have representation (upto 33 per cent of total) on Board of Directors of the domestic airline company.

- Government is planning to consider private sector participation in construction and operation of new airports on a BOT basis.

- Also minimum fleet size for a scheduled operator raised from the existing 3 aircrafts to 5.

- Management contract with a foreign airline is not permitted.

Potential

Construction of world class international airports in five cities, permitting upto 100% foreign equity investment announced.

Important private sector aided projects: New airport near Kochi (US $ 85.7 million), Projects for development of new airports at Bangalore and Mumbai and private sector participation are under consideration.

Other private sector aided airports that are planned are: Ahmedabad airport, Amritsar airport upgradation, Chennai cargo_ complex, new international terminal and a second runway for Delhi airport, runway extension and international block for Jaipur airport.

8.4 Conclusion

India has undertaken several concrete measures, in recent years, to attract Foreign Direct Investment in the country. An interesting fact to be noted here is that, among the investors, Mauritius and the US continued to be the largest sources of FDI in India in the late 90s. The reason for Mauritius being the favoured source of FDI into the country is the low income tax rates prevailing there.

In the current year 2000-2001, specific measures were taken for liberalising policies and streamlining procedures. At present all FDI are permitted under the automatic approval route, except for a small negative list. In a major effort to encourage investment in e-commerce, FDI upto 100 per cent has been permitted subject to specific conditions.

The existing upper limit of Rs. 1500 crore for FDI in projects involving electricity generation, transmission and distribution has been dispensed with. FDI under the automatic route has been permitted upto 100 per cent for all manufacturing activities (with certain exceptions) in Special Economic Zones (SEZs). Foreign equity participation of upto 26 per cent has been allowed in the insurance sector subject to the issue of necessary license by the Insurance Regulatory and Development Authority (IRDA). 100 per cent FDI has also been allowed in telecom sector.

The ongoing economic reforms in the area of foreign investment have improved India's attraction as a foreign destination in the perception of international community. The Global Competitiveness Report, 2000 released by World Economic Forum, Harvard University lists several encouraging parameters for the Indian economy as an investment destination.

Among the main competitive advantages of India highlighted by the report are licensing of technology, availability of suppliers, medium income tax rate, export promotion and quality of business environment. In the overall growth competitiveness ranking, India's position has improved to 49 in the year 2000 from 52 in 1999. To attract FDI from other countries, a wider liberalisation of the trade policy is under way.

Select Bibliography

Select Bibliography

Adndre, Sapir, "*Factors Influencing India's Export Performance*", Indian Council for Research and International Economic Relations, New Delhi, *Working Paper No.9* (1983).

Ahluwalia, Isher Judge, *Productivity and Growth in Indian Manufacturing* (London: Oxford University Press, 1991).

Asian Development Bank, *Towards Regional Co-operation in South Asia* (1987), Economics and Development Research Centre, ADB, Manila.

Bhagwati, Jagdish and Srinivasan, T.N., *Foreign Trade Regimes and Economic Development: India* (New York: National Bureau of Economic Research, 1975).

Bharadwaj (Ranganath), *Structural Basis of India's Foreign Trade* (Bombay: University of Bombay, 1962).

Chakravarty, S, *"Trade and Development: Some Basic Issues"*, International Social Science Journal, Vol. XXXV, No. 3. (1983).

Chakravarty, S., *"Development Experience in South Asia"*, Asian Development Review, Vol.6, No.1. (1988).

Da Costa, G.C., *India's Balance of Payments in the Seventies and the Eighties,* Himalaya Publishing House, 1990.

CMIE, *Monthly Review of the Indian Economy*, May 2001, Mumbai.

Dagli, Valilal, *India's Foreign Trade* (Vora and Company Publishers Private Limited, 1973).

Deo Raj Singh, *Pattern of Foreign Trade and Planning in India* (New Delhi: Criterion Publications, 1985).

Economic Survey, 2000-2001, Ministry of Finance, Government of India, New Delhi

GATT, *Country Study: India* (1994).

Ghosh Pradip K, *International Trade and Third World Development* (Cambridge University Press, USA, 1987).

Global Development Finance, 2000, The World Bank, Washington D.C. USA.

Government of India, *Industrial Policy Statement*, July 24, 1991.

Government of India, Planning Commission, *Eighth Five Year Plan*.

Government of India, Planning Commission, *Ninth Five Year Plan*.

Government of India, *Report of the Committee on Trade Policies*, 1984, New Delhi.

Indian Institute of Foreign Trade, *Global Economic Challenges in the New Millennium*, 1998.

International Financial Statistics, February 2001.

International Monetary Fund, *Balance of Payments Manual*, Washington, DC, 1977, p.408

Joseph and Susan Berk, *Total Quality Management* (Excel Books, 1993).

Manmohan Singh, *India's Export Trends and the Prospects for Self-sustained Growth* (London: Oxford University Press, 1964).

Ministry of Commerce, Annual Report, 1999-2000, New Delhi

Mukherjee, Neela, Mukherjee, Amitabha, *India's Foreign Trade by Regions* (Indus Publishing Company, 1988).

Nayyar, Deepak and Sen, Abhijit, *"International Trade and the Agricultural Sector in India"*, Economic and Political Weekly, May 14, 1994.

Pahariya, N.C., *Indian Exports, Structure and Determinants* (Delhi: Concept Publications, 1988).

Panchmukhi, V.R. and Brahamananda, *Development Process of the Indian Economy* (Bombay: Himalaya Publishing House, 1987).

Panchmukhi, V.R., *"Neglect of Economic Services"*, Economic Times, March 9, 1983.

Panchmukhi, V.R., Rao, L.L., Mukherji, I.N., *Economic Co-operation in the SAARC Region: Potential, Constraints and Policies* (Delhi: Concept Publications, 1990).

Panchmukhi, V.R., *Trade Policies of India: A Quantitative Analysis* (Delhi: Concept Publications, 1978).

Prabhu, P. P., *India's Trade Policy* (Indian Institute of Foreign Trade, 1998).

Raj Singh Deo, *Pattern of Foreign Trade and Planning in India* (Criterion Publishers, 1985).

Reserve Bank of India, *Report on Currency and Finance, 1999-2000*, Department of Economic Analysis and Policy, Mumbai.

SIA Newsletter, February 2001, Ministry of Industry, Government of India, New Delhi

Sainy, H. C., *India's Foreign Trade: Its Nature and Problems* (National Publishing House, 1979).

Singh, D.R., *"Proxy Effects of Market in India's Exports"*, Indian Economic Journal, January - March, 1983.

Sinha, Anup, *Economic Reforms and Macro Economic Policy*, Economic and Political Weekly, May, 16-23, 1994.

Tiwari, R.S. and Bhushri, N.K., *"World Trade Patterns: An Empirical Study of RCA Approach"*, India Quarterly Journal of International Affairs, 1987.

United Nations Conference on Trade and Development, *Trade and Development Report,* 1999.

World Economic Forum, *The Global Competitiveness Report, 1998.*

World Investment Report, 2000, United Nations, N.Y., USA.

World Trade and Development Report, 1999-2000, The World Bank, Washington, D.C., USA.

Yamazawa, Ippei, *Developing Economies in the Twenty-First Century: The Challenge of Globalisation*, 2000, Institute of Developing Economies, Japan.

Index

Index